Death and Immortality
in Middle-earth

Proceedings of The Tolkien Society
Seminar 2016

Edited by Daniel Helen

First published 2017 by Luna Press Publishing, Edinburgh
www.lunapresspublishing.com

ISBN-13: 978-1-911143-33-8

Cover illustration *The Second Sorrow of Túrin* copyright © 2016 by Peter Xavier Price

Published under the auspices of the Peter Roe Memorial Fund, seventeenth in the series.

Contents

iii

About the Peter Roe Memorial Fund

The Tolkien Society's seminar proceedings and other booklets are typically published under the auspices of the Peter Roe Memorial Fund, a fund in the Society's accounts that commemorates a young member who died in a traffic accident. Peter Roe, a young and very talented person joined the Society in 1979, shortly after his sixteenth birthday. He had discovered Middle-earth some time earlier, and was so inspired by it that he even developed his own system of runes, similar to the Dwarvish Angerthas, but which utilised logical sound values, matching the logical shapes of the runes. Peter was also an accomplished cartographer, and his bedroom was covered with multi-coloured maps of the journeys of the fellowship, plans of Middle-earth, and other drawings.

Peter was also a creative writer in both poetry and prose—the subject being incorporated into his own *Dwarvish Chronicles*. He was so enthusiastic about having joined the Society that he had written a letter ordering all the available back issues, and was on his way to buy envelopes when he was hit by a speeding lorry outside his home.

Sometime later, Jonathan and Lester Simons (at that time Chairman and Membership Secretary respectively) visited Peter's parents to see his room and to look at the work on which he had spent so much care and attention in such a tragically short life. It was obvious that Peter had produced, and would have continued to produce, material of such a high standard as to make a complete booklet, with poetry, calligraphy, stories and cartography. The then committee set up a special account in honour of Peter, with the consent of his parents, which would be the source of finance for the Society's special publications. Over the years a number of members have made generous donations to the fund.

The first publication to be financed by the Peter Roe Memorial Fund was *Some Light on Middle-earth* by Edward Crawford, published in 1985. Subsequent publications have been composed from papers delivered at Tolkien Society workshops and seminars, talks from guest speakers at the Annual Dinner, and collections of the best articles from past issues of *Amon Hen*, the Society's bulletin.

Dwarvish Fragments, an unfinished tale by Peter, was printed in *Mallorn* 15 (September 1980). A standalone collection of Peter's creative endeavours is currently being prepared for publication.

The Peter Roe Series

Conventions and Abbreviations

Citations to Tolkien's works are provided inline and use the following abbreviations. Because there are so many editions of *The Hobbit* and *The Lord of the Rings*, citations are by volume, book, and chapter only. Similarly, references to the appendices of *The Lord of the Rings* are by appendix, section, and subsection only. All other references are provided in footnotes according to the *MHRA Style Guide*. Bibliographies of all works consulted (other than Tolkien's works listed below) are found at the end of most chapters.

Arthur	*The Fall of Arthur,* ed. by Christopher Tolkien (London: HarperCollins, 2013; Boston: Houghton Mifflin Harcourt, 2013)
FR	*The Fellowship of the Ring*
Hobbit	*The Hobbit*
Letters	*The Letters of J.R.R. Tolkien,* ed. by Humphrey Carpenter with the assistance of Christopher Tolkien (London: George Allen & Unwin, 1981; Boston: Houghton Mifflin, 1981)
Lost Road	*The Lost Road and Other Writings*, ed. by Christopher Tolkien (London: Unwin Hyman, 1987; Boston: Houghton Mifflin, 1987)
Lost Tales I	*The Book of Lost Tales, Part One,* ed. by Christopher Tolkien (London: George Allen & Unwin, 1983; Boston: Houghton Mifflin, 1984)

Introduction

Daniel Helen

> I cordially dislike allegory in all its manifestations, and always
> have done so since I grew old and wary enough to detect
> its presence. I much prefer history, true or feigned, with its
> varied applicability to the thought and experience of readers.
> I think that many confuse 'applicability' with 'allegory'; but
> the one resides in the freedom of the reader, and the other in
> the purposed domination of the author. (*FR*, 'Foreword to the
> Second Edition')

Tolkien's rejection of allegorical and topical interpretations
of *The Lord of the Rings* is well-established. In the 'Foreword
to the Second Edition', he argued fervidly that the book has
no inner meaning and that the story would have been very
different had he intended it to be an allegory of the Second
World War. He made similar arguments in letters to readers
in the decade between the publication of *The Return of the
King* in 1955 and the second edition in 1965. In a draft letter to
Joanna de Bortandano in April 1956, he dismissed the notion
that his story was an allegory of atomic power.[1] But he did not
stop there. He revealed the theme that was most important to
him—as a reader rather than author:

> The real theme for me is about something much more
> permanent and difficult: Death and Immortality: the mystery

---

[1] In this letter, Tolkien initially toyed with the idea that *The Lord of the Rings*
was about 'Power' and 'Domination', but concluded that these themes merely
provide '"a setting" for characters to show themselves' (*Letters*, p. 246).

of the love of the world in the hearts of a race 'doomed' to leave and seemingly lose it; the anguish in the hearts of a race 'doomed' not to leave it, until its whole evil-aroused story is complete. (*Letters*, p. 246)

Although Tolkien repeats this view to other correspondents in further letters before 1965,[2] he did not include it in the 'Foreword to the Second Edition'. It is, however, implied. Having explained his objections to allegory, Tolkien nonetheless wrote that no author can be unaffected by their experience and provides the following personal example:

One has indeed personally to come under the shadow of war to feel fully its oppression; but as the years go by it seems now often forgotten that to be caught in youth by 1914 was no less hideous an experience than to be involved in 1939 and the following years. By 1918 all but one of my close friends were dead. (*FR*, 'Foreword to the Second Edition')

Tolkien did not set about to write a book about death, but the loss of his close friends during the First World War, compounded by the loss of both parents as a child, inevitably had a profound effect on him and helped shape his outlook on human mortality.

The present volume constitutes the proceedings of The Tolkien Society Seminar 2016. Held in Leeds on Sunday 2 July 2016, almost exactly 100 years after the start of the Battle of the Somme on 1 July 1916, the speakers were invited to present papers on the themes of life, death, and immortality in Tolkien's life and works. Thirteen presentations were delivered

---

[2] See letters 203, 208, and 211 (*Letters*, pp. 262, 267, 284). He also made a similar statement in *Tolkien in Oxford*, dir. by Leslie Megahey (BBC, 1968).

on the day, twelve of which are published here. The first paper, by Matthew B. Rose, provides a historical account of Tolkien's involvement in the Battle of the Somme. The following two papers explore some of the ways Tolkien's experience during the First World War influenced his writing. Comparing two very different authors, Tânia Azevedo shows how both Tolkien and T.S. Eliot turned to poetry to reflect on the absurdity and destruction of the Great War. Irina Metzler explores Tolkien's use of disabled characters in the context of changing attitudes towards disability following 1918 and the return of thousands of men left lame or maimed by war. We then turn to the theme of death more specifically. Giovanni Carmine Costabile breaks down the different ways characters respond to death—either the death of others or the prospect of their own—in *The Lord of the Rings*. Aslı Bülbül Candaş's paper considers death and immortality from the perspective of Elves, the viewpoint of much of Tolkien's writings on Middle-earth. Anna Milon exposes the irony behind the description of the Elves as 'immortal', which Tolkien portrays as serial longevity rather than exemption from death. Andrew Higgins demonstrates that Tolkien not only depicted concepts of life and death in his mythic narratives, but in his language development too. Sarah Rose examines the story of Arda's creation—comparing the Music of the Ainur to the ancient concept of universal symphony— to show that death was at first a gift from god before Melkor turned it into something evil. Turning to the perspective of Men, Gaëlle Abaléa highlights the use of transmission and memory as paths to immortality. The final three papers focus on different religious and theological aspects of Tolkien's legendarium. Analysing the Fall of not just Men but Elves and Ainur too, Massimiliano Izzo argues that death and deathlessness define the divide in the nature of the Fall between the two races of the Children of Ilúvatar. Drawing on the theology of spiritual formation, Adam B. Shaeffer describes the spiritual growth of Frodo, whose suffering is rewarded with admission to the Undying Lands, juxtaposed against the spiritual corruption of Saruman, whose fall leads to the loss (in a sense) of his immortality. Finally, Dimitra Fimi contends that the connection Tolkien draws between his theory of 'eucatastrophe' and the resurrection of Christ helps us understand why *The Lord of the Rings* leaves the reader feeling both joy and sorrow.

I am grateful to all the contributors of this collection for their hard work and patience. I would also like to acknowledge Verne Walker, without whom the 2016 seminar would not have been a success (and this book would not exist), together with Aurelie Bremont, who also presented on the day, and Shaun Gunner, who expertly chaired the event. The theme of death and immortality in Tolkien's writings is a relatively unexplored area in Tolkien studies.[3] Given its importance to Tolkien himself, it is hoped that this book will not only provide a meaningful contribution but will also encourage others to take the topic further.

---

[3] I am aware of only one other dedicated publication to date: *The Broken Scythe: Death and Immortality in the Works of J.R.R. Tolkien*, ed. by Roberto Arduini and Claudio A. Testi (Zurich and Jena: Walking Tree Publishers, 2012).

Tolkien and the Somme

Matthew B. Rose

Introduction

The twentieth century gave us splashes of light and deluges of darkness. At the dawn of the century came the First World War, the 'war to end all wars' which in its wake produced another world war and spread totalitarian communism throughout the world. In that 'Great War', technology, normally a tool for helping mankind, became a tool for man's destruction, weapons of slaughter. Across Europe, a generation of soldiers died; those who survived were, to borrow Yeats's line, 'Changed, changed utterly.'[1]

J.R.R. Tolkien was one such changed man. Tolkien lived through two world wars, but it was the First World War that profoundly affected his personal life and his writing, as it was during the Great War that Tolkien saw first-hand the carnage man could inflict on each other. Tolkien served in the Battle of the Somme, which lasted from 1 July–18 November 1916. To that end, we will begin by briefly looking at the history of World War I prior to the battle, move from there to a survey of the battle's four months, and conclude with some applications of the battle to Tolkien's life and works. This is a monumental topic, one which cannot be satisfactorily addressed in a short space. Yet try we must, for it is a story worth telling.[2]

---

[1] W.B. Yeats, 'Easter 1916', in *The Collected Poems of William Butler Yeats* (London: Wordsworth Editions, 2008), line 15.

[2] For a more in-depth study of this subject, see John Garth, *Tolkien and the Great War* (New York: Houghton Mifflin, 2003).

The War

On 28 June 1914, Archduke Franz Ferdinand, heir to the throne of the Austrian-Hungarian Empire, and his wife Sophie were assassinated in Sarajevo, Bosnia. Their deaths triggered a domino effect thanks to elaborate treaties and alliances in place among European nations. Words of warning were ignored as Germany sided with Austria-Hungary against Serbia and its allies. By the end of 1914, the major European powers (as well as the Ottoman Empire) found themselves at war with each other. Both sides seemed confident that they would prevail, that the war would end in a few short weeks, once the other side saw the military prowess of their opponents. As Kaiser Wilhelm II of Germany famously told his soldiers, they would return 'before the leaves have fallen from the trees.'[3]

He was almost comically wrong. Peace would not return until each country had spent its youth over four gruelling years. The strategies of earlier wars proved fallible in the wake of new technological weapons. The centuries-old strategy of sending lines of soldiers at opponents did not work well against the rapid fire of machine guns and heavy artillery. It is not surprising, then, that an attacking force, whether from the Allies or the Central Powers, faced overwhelmingly greater losses than the defenders.[4] Warren H. Carroll describes the situation in gripping detail:

Then came a new kind of horror. [...] The machine gun ruled

---

[3] Russell Freedman, *The War to End All Wars* (New York: Scholastic, 2010), p. 22.

[4] Hew Strachan, *The First World War* (New York: Penguin Books, 2003), pp. 164–65.

any fixed battlefield. There was no answer to it, no defense against it. Even a few days' stabilization of the battle-front, enough to permit machine guns to be emplaced in a system of trenches, made that front for all intents and purposes impregnable.[5]

Soldiers of both sides literally dug into the battlefield, and trenches traversed the European landscape. Mud and blood mixed, creating a horrific environment.

The overwhelming strategy for both sides was to pummel the opponent into submission. Victory meant forcing the other side to surrender through attrition, by slowly wearing down one's opponents until there was no one left to fight. Historian Michael Howard notes that armies became 'instruments through which the belligerents could bleed one another dry of resources and of men.'[6] Victory then was the few miles gained by the loss of millions of lives.

The western front in particular, situated along the barren boarder of France and Germany, provided the scene of an inhuman nightmare. The casualty lists of the battles stagger the imagination, seemingly impossible. An eighth of all British soldiers mobilized during the war never returned home. In 1915, the second year of the war, over five million men lost their lives as flesh and blood charged against the lead of the machine guns. By the middle of 1916, both sides feared a stalemate, and the push to gain land on both fronts became an obsession. At the Battle of Verdun (which lasted from February

---

[5] Warren H. Carroll, *The Rise and Fall of the Communist Revolution* (Front Royal, VA: Christendom Press, 1995), p. 57.

[6] Michael Howard, *War in European History* (Oxford: Oxford University Press, 1976), p. 114.

to December 1916, and shares with the Somme a well-deserved notoriety for the amount of blood spilled in one battle), over 262,000 men were either killed or reported missing. Perhaps most tragic of all, at the end of the battle, both sides were where they had started the battle; neither side had made a substantial advance in ten months.[7]

Verdun forced British general Sir Douglas Haig and French marshal Joseph Jacques Joffre to reassess plans to attack German forces along the Somme River; the new plan was to divert German attention from their attack on Verdun to the Somme, where both sides began to gather. The bloodiest battle of the war was about to commence.

The Battle

From the start, the Battle of the Somme was a military nightmare. Haig's original plan was a decisive victory against the Germans; that plan fell behind the more immediate goal of relieving pressure on the French troops at Verdun. The 'Big Push' to push back the German armies faltered. Haig's plan was an elaborate one, calling for prolonged bombing of the German positions for a week prior to the infantry charge. This would destroy any defences set up by the Germans, providing an easy route for the British soldiers.[8] It was a perfect plan,

---

[7] Carroll, *Rise and Fall*, p. 58.

[8] The artillery Haig requested did fire for a week prior to the Somme's commencement on 1 July. Unfortunately, many of the shells fired by the guns exploded prematurely, thereby not damaging the German defences. Those that did explode churned up the ground just ahead of the German position, making the earth susceptible to muddying with rain. See Daniel Grotta-Jurska, *J.R R. Tolkien: Architect of Middle-earth*, ed. by Frank Wilson

Haig felt; to his wife he wrote, 'I feel that every step in my plan has been taken with the Divine help.'[9] Unfortunately, Haig was a compromiser, and even when he felt strongly about a plan like the one he developed for the Somme, he tended to support dissenting views over his own.[10] While this view may be an asset in peaceful, political discussions, it is a shortcoming in times of war. An attack set for dawn was replaced by one at 7:30, almost three hours later. No matter when the attack came, the Germans would have been prepared for it, as the communication between British battalions was through radio contact, easily intercepted by the Germans.[11] They set up more barbed wire and machine gun nests, ready for the charge. The British soldiers had no additional defences while charging; indeed, they were expecting their pathways to be clear.

The result was 1 July 1916, the worst day of fighting in British military history, where the British suffered over 60,000 casualties.[12] Tolkien's biographer Humphrey Carpenter paints a grim picture of the fighting:

They scrambled up the ladders from the trenches and into the

(Philadelphia, PA: Running Press, 1976), p. 49.

[9] Quoted in Freedman, p. 94.

[10] One historian notes that, 'the accusation to be levelled against Haig was not so much that he was wrong to seek a breakthrough [at the Somme], for there were moments in the course of the battle when such opportunities beckoned, but that he failed to impose his vision on his subordinate commanders' (Strachan, p. 191).

[11] British soldiers made a disturbing discovery when they took the German position in Ovillers, a town near the Somme River: a 'verbatim transcript of the British orders to attack the village on July 1' (Garth, p. 172).

[12] Warren H. Carroll, *1917: Red Banners, White Mantle* (Front Royal, VA: Christendom College Press, 1984), p. 8.

open, forming up in straight lines as they had been instructed, and beginning their slow tramp forward—slow because each man was carrying at least sixty-five pounds of equipment. They had been told that the German defences were already virtually destroyed and the barbed wire cut by the Allied barrage. But they could see that the wire was not cut, and as they approached it the German machine-guns opened fire on them.[13]

The Allied forces became disorganized, bunching together rather than spreading out, thanks in large part to the strategic placement of the Germans' barbed wire.[14] They became even easier targets. 'We didn't have to aim,' a German machine-gunner wrote, 'we just fired into them.'[15]

The 'Great Push' strategy soon fizzled out, and the Battle of the Somme became another battle of attrition. As the battle raged onward, the likelihood of escaping alive dwindled. Historian Peter Hart notes the following:

Every time the men went forward into the front line they knew that there was a fair chance that they might never return. Whether they were holding the line or about to attack, they knew that their lives had reached a distinct crossroads. They hoped to survive unscathed, but they naturally feared death or the type of wound that would leave them crippled for life.[16]

---

[13] Humphrey Carpenter, *J.R.R. Tolkien: A Biography* (London: Unwin Paperbacks, 1978), p. 90.

[14] Grotta-Jurska, p. 49.

[15] Freedman, p. 97.

[16] Peter Hart, *The Somme: The Darkest Hour on the Western Front* (New York: Pegasus Books, 2008), p. 538.

The longer the battle lasted, the more chaotic the 'no-man's land' between the sides became. As one writer describes it,

> The horror increased daily. The rain and the shelling and the feet of thousands of men turned the land into a sea of mud. Most traces of vegetation disappeared and the trees that managed to remain standing looked like survivors of a forest fire—all leaves and bark stripped off or blown away. And there were corpses everywhere, bloated, stinking, disfigured or mutilated, with parts completely blown away.[17]

It was, to put it simply, hell.

As the long months dragged on, the deadening stalemate begged for a creative solution. Haig found one in a newly arrived technological wonder: the Mark I tank. The Mark I did not have the finesse of tanks used during World War II. It had two purposes: force a path through the barbed wire chaos of 'no-man's land' and terrify the Germans. It did this through a combination of crawling across the ground at about four miles an hour, blasting and shooting obstacles with its formidable machine and 6-pounder guns.[18] The tank proved mediocre at their first task (the tanks did crush through the barbed wire, but in the process the tanks churned up the muddy ground, often getting themselves trapped in the process, and were soon stopped by either German artillery fire or mechanical breakdown) and temporarily successful at the second. On their first day of use (15 September), for example, the tanks led the British to gain 3,500 yards before breaking down.[19] One

[17] Katharyn W. Crabbe, *J.R.R. Tolkien* (New York: Continuum, 1988), p. 14.

[18] Hart, p. 363.

[19] Freedman, p. 99.

British soldier's description of the tanks' first outing highlights the successes and failures of the new technology. The tanks at first were stuck firing at the British, rather than the Germans; however, once the tank operators got their bearings, they advanced onto the German line, 'frightening the Jerries out of their wits and making them scuttle like frightened rabbits.'[20] Haig was impressed and used more of tanks in the British attacks; however, the Germans soon got used to the tanks after discovering their susceptibility to artillery fire, and the war of attrition continued.

Eventually, in mid-November, the German forces withdrew from the Somme. At the same time, British and French troops 'officially called off' their attack.[21] It was a 'victory' for the Allies, and the victory justified not only the Somme, but also the other battles of attrition that scarred 1916.[22] The casualty numbers still stagger the mind: over 1.4 million casualties. Warren H. Carroll writes,

> On the Somme River, in the summer of 1916, over 600,000 British and French soldiers were killed or wounded to gain just eight miles, and 650,000 Germans were killed or wounded to limit them to that. Those eight miles cost the life or health of thirty men for every foot, two and a half men for every inch.[23]

This battle, more than any other part of the war, shaped the young John Ronald Reuel Tolkien.

[20] Bert Chaney, 'The First Tanks in Action, 15 September 1916', in *Eyewitness to History*, ed. by John Carey (New York: Avon Books, 1987), pp. 466–67 (p. 467).

[21] Freedman, p. 99.

[22] Strachan, p. 196.

[23] Carroll, *Rise and Fall*, p. 58.

The Man

The years that spanned the First World War transformed the young John Ronald Tolkien. As war was brewing, his childhood sweetheart and future wife Edith entered the Catholic Church, a requirement before she and the Catholic John Ronald could be betrothed.[24] Tolkien was a student at Oxford at the time, eventually focusing on English language and literature. As his fellow students joined the British military, Tolkien remained at Oxford to finish his studies. It was not for lack of patriotism that he remained home; on the contrary, it was for security. If he were to enter the army having completed his schooling at Oxford, he would be well equipped to find employment after the war in the field he desired and, at the same time, provide for his expectant family.[25]

A few years prior to the war, prior to attending Oxford, Tolkien had formed a close group of friends at King Edward's School. They named themselves the TCBS, the 'Tea Club and Barrovian Society', after their habit of meeting for tea and conversation in the school's library and in the Barrow Stores in town. The four friends (Tolkien, Rob Gilson, G.B. Smith, and Christopher Wiseman) soon gathered around them other students at the school; however, these four remained closest, the core of the TCBS.[26] After they graduated from King Edward's, their paths diverged: Tolkien and Smith went to Oxford, while Gilson and Wiseman went to Cambridge. However, they frequently exchanged letters, even occasionally

---

[24] Carpenter, p. 76.

[25] Carpenter, p. 80; Grotta-Kurska, p. 41.

[26] Of the four, Tolkien and Wiseman were at first closest. They referred to each other as the 'Two Great Brethren.

meeting together. Key among these meetings was the 'Council of London.' There the mission of the TCBS was refined, with focus placed on the Society's mission of transforming the world for God and truth; there in London, Tolkien found encouragement from his friends for his poetry.[27]

The TCBS was for Tolkien a sort of predecessor of the Inklings, and if the TCBS prefigures the comradery of the Inklings, then G.B. Smith's shared love of poetry and Christopher Wiseman's encouragement and suggestions to Tolkien about the latter's sub-creations prefigures the relationship between C.S. Lewis and Tolkien.[28] Christopher Wiseman in particular encouraged Tolkien in the later years of World War I to continue working on the mythology that would eventually become Tolkien's legendarium.[29]

Britain's declaration of war called an entire generation of men to arms. The TCBSites were no exception. All four of them served in the military. Tolkien joined with the Lancashire Fusiliers (first the 13th Battalion, then eventually the 11th) soon after his graduation from Oxford in July 1915 and his marriage to Edith on 22 March 1916.[30] That year, 1916, was one of the most tumultuous of Tolkien's life.[31] It was during

---

[27] See Garth, pp. 59, 231 for the effect of the TCBS on Tolkien's poetry and p. 137 for more on the mission of the TCBS.

[28] *Ibid.*, pp. 281–82.

[29] *Ibid.*, p. 224.

[30] The 13th Battalion was more of a reserve battalion, a reservoir of soldiers, established to replace soldiers lost in combat. See Garth, p. 94.

[31] Tolkien later wrote to his son Christopher how he had 'produced a First in Finals in 1915. Bolted into the army: July 1915. I found the situation intolerable and married on March 22, 1916. May found me crossing the Channel (I still have the verse I wrote on the occasion!) for the carnage of the Somme' (*Letters*, p. 53).

this year that he would experience the 'animal horror', as he would later call it, of war.[32]

Tolkien arrived in France on 5 June 1916. Since he preferred, as Carpenter puts it, the 'prospect of dealing with words, messages and codes' more than the 'drudgery and responsibility of commanding a platoon', Tolkien trained to be the signal officer for his battalion.[33] His knowledge of the codes used by the army allowed him to develop his own code to send messages of his locations to Edith, who kept a map of Europe on the wall, with which she tracked his battalion's movements.[34]

Tolkien and his battalion were not yet at the Somme on 1 July; however, Tolkien still faced the effects of the battle. In that initial charge on 1 July, Tolkien's friend and fellow TCBSite Rob Gilson died, a loyal soldier to the end.[35] It was through the other TCBSites that Tolkien heard of his friend's death. Smith and Wiseman took the news of Gilson's death better than Tolkien did; not that they did not mourn for the loss of one of their own, but rather that they saw hope in the darkness. Tolkien saw in Gilson's death the end of the TCBS. Both Smith and Wiseman disagreed. Smith described Gilson to Tolkien as, 'gone from among us' yet 'still altogether with us.'[36] Wiseman likewise wrote to Smith about Gilson: 'It is by no means nonsense, though we have no reason to suppose, that Rob is still of the TCBS. But I believe there is something

[32] Carpenter, p. 91.

[33] *Ibid*, pp. 85–86.

[34] Garth, p. 207.

[35] *Ibid.*, pp. 155–56.

[36] Quoted in Garth, p. 179.

in what the Church calls the Communion of Saints.'[37] It took the friendship of Wiseman and Smith to remind Tolkien that friendship does not end in this life, that it lives on into eternity.

It would not be the last time the TCBS suffered loss during the war. Shortly after the Battle of the Somme, Smith died from an infected shrapnel wound. Tolkien took this loss worse than he did the loss of Rob Gilson. John Garth writes,

> It was for G. B. Smith that Tolkien mourned most deeply; the two had understood each other's social background and maternal upbringing; they had shared a school, a university, a regiment, and a bloody page of history; they had been akin in their reverence for poetry and the imagination and had spurred each other into creative flight.[38]

In short, they were like what the ancient Irish called an 'Anam Cara', a sort of friend so close as to be like soulmates, a sort of 'soul friend'. His death gave Tolkien 'an even greater duty to carry on their jointly conceived project, which was to do God's will in the world.'[39]

14 July saw Tolkien and the 11th Lancashire Fusiliers' first day of fighting during the Somme; they took part in retrieving the town of Ovillers. As a signal officer, Tolkien remained towards the rear of the action. That does not, of course, mean his role was negligible. On the contrary, as John Garth states, 'In this war of men and machines, the infantry counted little, the artillery rather more, and the word most of all: without fast

---

[37] Quoted in Garth, p. 185.

[38] Garth, p. 250.

[39] Bradley Birzer, *J.R.R. Tolkien's Sanctifying Myth: Understanding Middle-earth* (Wilmington, DE: ISI Books, 2003), pp. 2, 46.

and accurate communications, no one could hope to have the upper hand.'[40] After two days of fighting, the Allies had taken Ovillers, thanks in large part to Tolkien.

Tolkien's battalion would be involved in several other attacks before the Battle of the Somme ended in November. Tolkien, however, was not in the mood to celebrate. Although he had served valiantly during the battle, and was assuredly glad the fighting there was over, Tolkien had another, more immediate issue: his health. On 27 October, barely a week after the 11th Lancashire Fusiliers' final attack during the Battle of the Somme (at Regina Trench), Lieutenant Tolkien went to the medical officer, feeling 'weak and unwell'; he had a high fever, later determined to be 'trench fever', a bacterial infection spread by lice.[41] In the best-case scenario, the victim suffered from headaches, pain in the back and legs, and a rash; more severe cases sometimes ended in heart failure. Either way, Tolkien needed to get away from the front lines to recuperate. As many commentators and Tolkien biographers have noted, this infection saved his life. No longer would he be in the line of fire. No longer would he face the threat of German artillery or machine guns. He had, for the first time in many months, time to write.

And write he did. It was during this time of recuperation that Tolkien began, in earnest, to fashion his legendarium. He would do this throughout the rest of the war as he was transferred to various stations in England following his return home on 8 November 1916. While in and out of the hospital (it took years for the trench fever to final leave him), Tolkien

---

[40] Garth, p. 165.
[41] *Ibid*, p. 200.

would compose tales, drawing from his scholarly interests and his experiences in war. The result was *The Book of Lost Tales*, the precursor for *The Silmarillion*.

When the war ended, Lieutenant Tolkien (he had been promoted to full lieutenant since returning to England) sought a job. His plan of completing his degree before enlisting paid off, and in 1918 he began working for the *Oxford English Dictionary*. In the coming years, he became a professor at the University of Leeds and eventually at Oxford. All the while, the Great War and the scarring Battle of the Somme remained with him, inspiring his sub-creation.

His Mythology

Tolkien was always emphatic that he did not create his legendarium as an allegory for the world war (neither the first, nor the second one). Nor should one claim that World War I was the sole influence on Tolkien's mythology. His Roman Catholic faith and his love of medieval literature had comparably important roles. However, as biographer Joseph Pearce notes, Tolkien's 'experience of the "animal horror" darkened his vision to such an extent that the shadow of the First World War always lingers, vulturelike, over his work.'[42]

Some of the effects of the Great War on the legendarium are subtler than others. For example, Tolkien stated that he modelled the brave and loyal Samwise Gamgee after the batmen, the common English soldier that Tolkien preferred to spend his time with while on the front.[43] Even Sam's name is

---

[42] Joseph Pearce, *Literary Giants, Literary Catholics* (San Francisco, CA: Ignatius Press, 2005), p. 242.

[43] Carpenter, p. 89. Of the characteristics and duties of the batmen, see Garth,

derived from the war: his surname Gamgee is derived from Dr Gamgee, which Tolkien connected to the type of bandages used during the war, but John Garth also connected to a surgeon who took care of Tolkien when he had returned to England (*Letters*, p. 179).[44] Tolkien also noted that the churned, barren ground of Mordor and the lifeless limbo of the Dead Marshes 'owe something to' the Somme (*Letters*, p. 303). It does smack of the 'no-man's land' between enemies in France.[45]

The Somme had a more direct effect, however, on earlier incarnations of the mythology, particularly in *The Book of Lost Tales*, and most especially in 'The Fall of Gondolin'. Tolkien had little time to write while in France; his time in hospitals after contracting 'trench fever' presented an opportunity to develop the stories that until then had danced around in his imagination (*Letters*, p. 78).[46] It was because of this that 'The Fall of Gondolin', the first of these tales, came out 'fully formed' as Tolkien himself said (*Letters*, p. 215).

John Garth points to several aspects of the tale that indicate influences of World War I in general and the Battle of the Somme in particular. We will focus on only one aspect of the story, the weaponized dragons used by the evil Melko (the precursor of Melkor/Morgoth in *The Silmarillion*) and the Orcs to attack Gondolin, the city of the Gnomes (the precursors of the Noldor Elves).

Tolkien knew well the attributes of Germanic dragons,

---

p. 171.

[44] See also Garth, p. 206.

[45] Birzer, pp. 2–3.

[46] Birzer notes that 'Christopher Tolkien confirms that extant pieces of *The Silmarillion* and the larger mythology appear on the back of official army documents dating from the war' (Birzer, p. 31).

particularly as found in *Beowulf* (Old English) and the stories of Fafnir (Old Norse).[47] Tolkien knew how dragons were greedy, had hard scaly skin with a weak spot on their underbelly (think the chink in the armour of Smaug). He knew they usually breathed fire or poison and that they were sometimes supernatural products of greed, symbolized by the 's obsession with its gold hoard.

The dragons that appear in 'The Fall of Gondolin' are similar to Fafnir and Beowulf's bane. With them, however, Tolkien takes the typical Germanic dragon motif and transforms it. These dragons are more machines than monsters. They are fully armoured without the typical Germanic dragon's soft underside. Some of them carry Orc soldiers inside, some spew fire. They cross the churned ground smoothly, undeterred, 'like slow rivers of metal' (*Lost Tales II*, p. 170). It does not take much imagination to see the inspiration of the Mark I tanks, which carried soldiers inside their metal bodies and rolled over the battlefield using belts rather than wheels.[48] Like the tanks, the mechanical dragons force their way through Gondolin's defences, crushing their barriers, winning the battle for Melko. They demonstrate a greater theme found throughout Tolkien's work: using machines for evil purposes, particularly to slaughter and destroy. Machines and artificial creatures are the favoured tools of Melko/Morgoth and his successor Sauron. However, we should be hesitant to draw a one-to-one comparison. The fact that Melko uses the dragon tanks, while at the Battle of the Somme the English used the real tanks,

---

[47] Tolkien referred to these two dragons as the 'only two that are significant' in medieval literature in his famous lecture '*Beowulf*: The Monsters and the Critics'.

[48] Garth, pp. 220–21.

emphasizes that Tolkien's stories never perfectly match his biographical experiences.[49]

Tolkien survived the horrors of World War I with the mission to bring truth to the world, as his friends in the TCBS had vowed to do. While the Great War and the Battle of the Somme do not provide a key to all of Tolkien's work, it does allow us a glimpse into the mythology's genesis. Despite the darkness of war and the horrific battle begun a century ago, this past century produced one of the greatest stories in our western canon. Good comes from evil whether through the hand of God or by the imagination of sub-creators like Tolkien. Perhaps that is, ultimately, the lesson we can draw from the horrors of World War I, the Somme, and the courage of J.R.R. Tolkien.

---

[49] *Ibid.*, p. 220.

Works Consulted

Birzer, Bradley, *J.R.R. Tolkien's Sanctifying Myth: Understanding Middle-earth* (Wilmington, DE: ISI Books, 2003)

Carey, John, ed., *Eyewitness to History* (New York: Avon Books, 1987)

Carpenter, Humphrey, *J.R.R. Tolkien: A Biography* (London: Unwin Paperbacks, 1978)

Carroll, Warren H., *1917: Red Banners, White Mantle* (Front Royal, VA: Christendom College Press, 1984)

——, *The Rise and Fall of the Communist Revolution* (Front Royal, VA: Christendom Press, 1995)

Crabbe, Katharyn W., *J.R.R. Tolkien* (New York: Continuum, 1988)

Freedman, Russell, *The War to End All Wars* (New York: Scholastic, 2010)

Garth, John, *Tolkien and the Great War: The Threshold of Middle-earth* (New York: Houghton Mifflin, 2003)

Grotta-Jurska, Daniel, *J.R R. Tolkien: Architect of Middle-earth*, ed. by Frank Wilson (Philadelphia, PA: Running Press, 1976)

Hart, Peter, *The Somme: The Darkest Hour on the Western Front* (New York: Pegasus Books, 2008)

Howard, Michael, *War in European History* (Oxford: Oxford University Press, 1976)

Pearce, Joseph, *Literary Giants, Literary Catholics* (San Francisco, CA: Ignatius Press, 2005)

Strachan, Hew, *The First World War* (New York: Penguin Books, 2003)

Yeats, W.B., *The Collected Poems of William Butler Yeats* (London: Wordsworth Editions, 2008)

Tolkien and T.S. Eliot:
the waste land and a fallen king

Tânia Azevedo

At a first glance, it seems hard to find connections between T.S. Eliot and J.R.R. Tolkien. They lived during roughly the same period and even shared Oxford as a common living area for a while. Did they know each other? At least on paper, yes. In person, they probably met once or twice, but as far as we know, they did not really know each other. However, at the end of the First World War—where both lost friends, acquaintances and saw the map of Europe change—both of them chose to reflect on the destruction of war, already in a time of peace:

> One has indeed personally to come under the shadow of war to feel fully its oppression; but as the years go by it seems now often forgotten that to be caught in youth by 1914 was no less hideous an experience than to be involved in 1939 and the following years. By 1918, all but one of my close friends were dead. (*FR*, 'Foreword to the Second Edition')

In the 1920s, Eliot composed his poem *The Waste Land* and Tolkien wrote (although it was only published in 2013) the incomplete poem *The Fall of Arthur*. My aim is to show how both texts search for healing in the wounded land and the wounded mankind, although both works ultimately fail to reach this objective. I argue all that remains is the trauma and memory of loss in Tolkien and a feeble hope of change in Eliot.

How, then, can we compare two authors whose works diverge so much? We need to go back into the past to their common link, C.S. Lewis. The literary group Tolkien belonged to—the 'Inklings'—had as one of its members C.S. Lewis, a renowned author and also friends with Tolkien. C.S. Lewis had a feud with T.S. Eliot simply because he did not appreciate what Eliot wrote about and how he did it. It was actually a clash of literary views and currents. Lewis would use his classes to show Eliot's texts as an example of 'bad literature' and he even called it 'trash' to modernism. He would also use the Inklings meetings to convey his opinions on Eliot as he read his poems out loud and publicly explained what he disliked about them. Lewis even dedicated three pages of his 1942 work *A Preface to Paradise* Lost exclusively to attack Eliot's ideas and works.

T.S. Eliot, on the other hand, only replied politely to such attacks. He even tried to improve their relationship when their common friend Charles Williams passed away in 1945. Tolkien, apparently, also did not appreciate Eliot's works, but this seems to be connected with the almost dogmatic issues that surrounded the organization of the syllabus of English literature at the University of Oxford. Tolkien worked with Lewis in developing the course and both wanted all examples of modernism banned from it. However, when Eliot died in 1965, Tolkien, in a letter dated 9 January, wrote that the eight-verse poem dedicated to him by John Masefield in *The Times* was 'a perfect specimen of bad verse' (*Letters*, p. 353).[1]

---

[1] John Masefield, 'East Coker', *Poetry Explorer* (1965) <http://www.poetryexplorer.net/poem.php?id=10105230> [accessed 13 October 2017]:

Here, whence his forbears sprang, a man is laid
As dust, in quiet earth, whose written word
Helped many thousands broken and dismayed
Among the ruins of triumphant wrong.
May many an English flower and little bird

Perhaps he thought that Eliot, as a good poet, might deserve something better.

Bearing all of this in mind, one should not expect that two authors who worked in such diverse fields—Tolkien in fantasy and Eliot in modernism—could have something in common, particularly in texts that were produced so early in their careers. However, it is in these two poems—*The Waste Land* and *The Fall of Arthur*—that both authors reflect on war in a time of peace and portray a wounded land that looks for healing. My aim is not to analyse these poems, but to show the relevant verses to identify the thematic similarities between the two texts.

Parallels

In the first section of Eliot's *The Waste Land*, 'The Burial of the Dead', we actually see what the title says. After the war, we need to bury not only the dead but the painful memories. But death left desolation, emptiness, silence:

> What are the roots that clutch, what branches grow
> Out of this stony rubbish? [...]
> dead trees give no shelter
> dry stone no sound of water. Only
> There is shadow under this red rock. [...]
> I will show you fear in a handful of dust.
> [...] I was neither
> Living nor dead, and I knew nothing,

(Primrose and robin redbreast unafraid)
Gladden this garden where his rest is made
And Christmas song respond, and Easter song.

Looking into the heart of light, the silence.[2]

In *The Fall of Arthur*, Tolkien presents us a King Arthur whose life is declining, someone who knows he has to face a last battle for the healing of his land. He rides east against the enemy but, while doing it, he contemplates his kingdom, a wasteland, empty, wounded:

> waste was behind them, | | walls before them;
> on the houseless hills | | ever higher mounting
> vast, unvanquished, | | lay the veiled forest.
> Dark and dreary | | were the deep valleys,
> where limbs gigantic | | of lowering trees
> in endless ailes | | were arched o'er rivers
> flowing down afar | | from fells of ice.
> [...] Fear clutched their souls,
> waiting watchful | | in a world of shadow
> for woe they knew not, | | no word speaking
> (*Arthur*, pp. 19–20, 22)

In the second section of his poem, 'A Game of Chess', Eliot describes a feminine character who is unique:

> Under the firelight, under the brush, her hair
> Spread out in fiery points
> Glowed into words, then would be savagely still.[3]

We are immediately reminded how Tolkien, in his poem,

---

[2] T.S. Eliot, The Waste Land (Urbana, Illinois: Project Gutenberg, 1998) <http://www.gutenberg.org/ebooks/1321> [accessed 13 October 2017], I. 20–21, 24–26, 31, 39–42.

[3] *Ibid.*, II. 108–110.

describes Guinevere and the evil effects of her betrayal:

> […] lady ruthless,
> Fair as fay-woman | | and fell-minded
> In the world walking | | for the woe of men.[4]
> (*Arthur*, p. 37)

In the third section of Eliot's text, 'The Fire Sermon', we are once again brought to the desolation and the expectation that nothing, according to the poetic subject, will come for sure:

> […] The wind
> Crosses the brown land, unheard. The nymphs are departed.
> Sweet Thames, run softly, till I end my song. […]
> I can connect
> Nothing with nothing
> The broken fingernails of dirty hands
> My people humble people who expect
> Nothing.[5]

In Tolkien's work, it is Arthur himself who announces his fate:

> Now from hope's summit | | headlong falling
> his heart foreboded | | that his house was doomed,
> the ancient world | | to its end falling
> and the tides of time | | turned against him.
> (*Arthur*, p. 24)

In the fifth section of Eliot's poem, there are two excerpts which are essential to the point I wish to make. The first has to

---

[4] A clear echo of Grendel's mother in *Beowulf*.

[5] *The Waste Land*, III. 174–76, 301–06.

do with the 'Fisher King' as a character.[6] This can be directly related to the medieval Arthurian material and also to Tolkien's text where we see a King Arthur who ardently wishes to heal his land but also knows that it will not be his hand that will provide the cure.

Eliot:

> I sat upon the shore
> Fishing, with the arid plain behind me
> Shall I at least set my lands in order?[7]

Tolkien:

> [...] Now pity whelmed him
> and love of his land | | and his loyal people,
> for the low mislead | | and the long-tempted,
> the weak that wavered, | | for the wicked grieving. [...]
> he would pass in peace | | pardon granting,
> the hurt healing | | and the whole guiding,
> to Britain the blessed | | bliss recalling.
> (*Arthur*, pp. 56–57)

Eliot versus Tolkien

The second moment in Eliot's text I would like to underline is:

> He who was living is now dead
> We who were living are now dying

---

[6] Connected to Chrétien's and Boron's texts. Eliot also searched for inspiration in Jessie Weston's *From Ritual to Romance*.
[7] *The Waste Land*, v. 423–25.

With a little patience.[8]

These verses can be connected to the final lament of Arthur in Tolkien's poem (which has not seen the light of publication and only reached the reader through Christopher Tolkien's notes) that, in my opinion, stresses the fall of the king. This is the lament for Gawain's death, his champion, the only defender of the kingdom:

> now my glory is gone | | and my grace[9] ended.
> Here lies my hope and my help | | and my helm and my sword
> my heart and my hardihood | | and my … of strength
> my counsel and comfort […]
> Ah, dread death | | thou dwellest too long,
> thou drownest my heart | | ere I die.
> (*Arthur*, p. 131)

I have left to the end the moments in these two poems that show differences rather than similarities. In Tolkien's text there is a feeling of impending loss. The reader knows, from early in the poem that the healing of the land and the people is not possible. Death comes to Arthur from the sea, by the hand of his enemies. The kingdom will be over. However, in section four of Eliot's poem, 'Death by Water', we see something different. Although we might at first interpret these verses as a warning about the inevitability of death, they could also be interpreted as rebirth, something akin to baptism where the 'old man' dies

---

[8] *The Waste Land*, v. 328–30.

[9] 'good' is written above 'grace' in the original manuscript and is probably meant as a potential replacement rather than a potential addition.

in the water and the 'new man' emerges:

> Phlebas the Phoenician, a fortnight dead,
> Forgot the cry of gulls, and the deep sea swell
> And the profit and loss.
> A current under sea
> Picked his bones in whispers. As he rose and fell
> He passed the stages of his age and youth
> Entering the whirlpool.
> Gentile or Jew
> O you who turn the wheel and look to windward,
> Consider Phlebas, who was once handsome and tall as you.[10]

As E.L. Risden wrote, 'it suggests more a baptism than another death: after the war we must cleanse and rebuild, regardless of how painful the process.'[11]

Some questions

Does Eliot go, then, beyond Tolkien searching for healing for the trauma of war? He seems to know the solution has to be an inner change of mankind so that devastation does not succeed again.

> Those divergent works exhibit rather extraordinary parallel concerns with the landscapes of end-times in personal, social,

---

[10] *The Waste Land*, IV. 312–21.

[11] E.L. Risden, 'Middle-earth and the Waste Land: Greenwood, Apocalypse, and Post-War Resolution', in *Tolkien in the New Century: Essays in Honor of Tom Shippey*, ed. by John Wm. Houghton, Janet Brennan Croft, Nancy Martsch, John D. Rateliff and Robin Anne Reid (Jefferson: McFarland, 2014), pp. 57–77 (p. 59).

and cosmic terms. Significant commonalities emerge through various lenses—for instance, through extreme landscapes, concerns with hidden brutalities, and culturally precipitous moments. […] Both *The Waste Land* and Tolkien's fiction find their particularity in non-realistic approaches to fully realistic feelings and ideas - and in the writers' responses to post-war devastation both physical, in the landscape of Europe, and emotional, in the suffering of nations worldwide.[12]

These responses seem to be different though. T.S. Eliot seems to devise hope in an inner change of mankind. In Tolkien's text, however, and probably due to its incomplete state, we can only see the fall, the devastation, and the end of an era of heroes, prosperity and victory. It is a chant of the lost kingdom and heroes. In Eliot, death by water is necessary but in Tolkien it is inevitable and a point of no return. In Eliot, the cycles of nature seem to be the warranty of renovation and in Tolkien the land is fatally wounded like the king and, because of that, has no possible cure. It is possible that in Tolkien the memory of the trauma is the solution. Perhaps through the persistency of memory mankind might avoid the errors of the past. Unfortunately, this has not happened, and Tolkien has, once again, to remember the First World War when his sons enlist in Second World War. In a letter to his youngest son, Christopher, who was in South Africa during the war, Tolkien criticised the human ability to so quickly forget the destruction of war: 'But so short is human memory and so evanescent are its generations that in about 30 years there will be few or no people with that direct experience, which alone goes really to the heart' (*Letters*, pp. 75–76).

---

[12] *Ibid.*

Works Consulted

Eliot, T.S., *The Waste Land* (Urbana, Illinois: Project Gutenberg, 1998) <http://www.gutenberg.org/ebooks/1321> [accessed 13 October 2017]

Masefield, John, 'East Coker', *Poetry Explorer* (1965) <http://www.poetryexplorer.net/poem.php?id=10105230> [accessed 13 October 2017]

Risden, E.L., 'Middle-earth and the Waste Land: Greenwood, Apocalypse, and Post-War Resolution', in *Tolkien in the New Century: Essays in Honor of Tom Shippey*, ed. by John Wm. Houghton, Janet Brennan Croft, Nancy Martsch, John D. Rateliff and Robin Anne Reid (Jefferson: McFarland, 2014), pp. 57–77

Tolkien and disability: the narrative function of disabled characters in Middle-earth

Irina Metzler

J.R.R. Tolkien's narrative use of disabled characters in his literary works may be treated in three themes: firstly, by looking at current definitions of disability and impairment; secondly, Tolkien's experience of the First World War as part of a wider development in how modern warfare and concepts of disability were linked; and thirdly, by performing a series of literary case studies of disabled characters in Tolkien's texts.

Definitions of disability and impairment

Modern theories of disability and disability studies cannot be understood without something commonly referred to as the social model of disability. According to this model, impairment and disability are seen as two different categories:

Impairment:

Lacking part or all of a limb, or having a defective limb, organ, or mechanism of the body.

Disability:

The disadvantage or restriction of activity caused by a contemporary social organisation which takes no or little account of people who have physical impairments and thus excludes them from the mainstream of social activities.[1]

What most disability studies theorists have in common is an emphasis on the distinction between the social construction of disability and the physiological reality of impairment. The distinction is absolutely vital. In very much simplified terms, according to the social model of disability, impairment is the anatomical, biological, physical condition that affects a person's body; it is a somatic condition. Disability is a social construct that is laid on top of this somatic condition. You are perhaps born impaired, but it is society that makes you disabled. Armed with the distinction between impairment and disability, the historian or literary critic can then set off on the discovery of disability in past times and texts, and can find how, why, and in what way impaired people may or may not have been regarded as disabled by their cultures.

Some of these attitudes were shaped by concepts of health and illness, prompting the question where disability fits into this dyad. Is disability an illness? Disability may be described as a liminal state, since the disabled person is situated between health and illness. Liminality, in its meaning of being on the border, in-between, not one or the other, has proved a useful concept when discussing medieval notions of (physical) impairment.[2] What is crucial for the argument here is the liminal state of the disabled person: neither ill nor healthy, they fit in neither category. Therefore, disability also fits with neither death nor immortality, which formed the main themes of The Tolkien Society Seminar 2016, precisely because disability is a state of being in limbo. More prosaically, the disabled person

---

[1] C. Barnes, G. Mercer and T. Shakespeare, *Exploring Disability: A Sociological Introduction* (Cambridge: Polity Press, 1999), p. 28.

[2] Irina Metzler, *Disability in Medieval Europe* (London: Routledge, 2006).

is neither healthy nor ill, neither well nor sick. This liminal position of disability is what makes disability problematic, both to modern theorists and the medical profession.

Liminality was indirectly alluded to by a fellow participant at the 2016 seminar, Tânia Azevedo, who looked at the literary linkages between Tolkien's *The Fall of Arthur* and T.S. Eliot's *The Waste Land*. Pertinent on the liminality of the disabled here is the line 'I was neither living nor dead' which occurs as a phrase in Eliot.[3]

Furthermore, disability is a static as opposed to dynamic condition. In addition to thinking about liminality, one may also define the difference between illness, sickness or disease on the one hand, and impairment or disability on the other hand, as the difference between dynamic and static states. According to medical thinking, illness has an evolution, since every illness from which someone recovers passes from onset, through intensification, to stasis, to recovery. By this definition, illness is a dynamic condition, changing and evolving to take one or the other course. Impairment, irrespective of causes, whether accidentally acquired or congenital, is a static condition, unchanging and permanently present. But in modern, western medicine the predominant view is that illness, and hence disability, according to the medical model, has to follow a restitution narrative: a patient is expected to say 'yesterday I was well, today I am ill, but tomorrow I will be better'. The disabled person fits neither model, since the functional loss

---

[3] See the essay on Tolkien and Eliot by E.L. Risden, 'Middle-earth and the Waste Land: Greenwood, Apocalypse, and Post-War Resolution', in *Tolkien in the New Century: Essays in Honor of Tom Shippey*, ed. by John Wm. Houghton, Janet Brennan Croft, Nancy Martsch, John D. Rateliff and Robin Anne Reid (Jefferson: McFarland, 2014), pp. 57–64.

renders a body not truly healthy, yet the disabled person never recovers that loss.

War and disability

The theme of disability was not directly related to the emphasis on death and immortality with regard to the 2016 commemoration of Tolkien and the Great War. However, I want to add a historiographic preamble on the history of disability as being something that is directly linked to the large numbers of maimed and mutilated veterans of the First World War returning home. One need only look to the aftermath of the war, when hundreds of thousands of soldiers on both sides of the conflict returned home shell-shocked, blinded, amputated and dreadfully mutilated in too many ways to describe. The extent of disability among these veterans as a consequence especially of mutilated limbs leading to large numbers of very noticeable crippled veterans has been discussed by modern historians.[4]

The impact of the First World War, and especially the publicly visible, large numbers of maimed soldiers returning from the front, prompted academic as well as medical interest in disability and rehabilitation. The decade immediately after the Great War produced a variety of articles, tracts and monographs

---

[4] See the chapter on the consequences of 'Mutilation' in Joanna Burke, *Dismembering the Male: Men's Bodies, Britain and the Great War* (London: Reaktion, 1996), especially at pp. 31–33; also Seth Koven, 'Remembering and Dismemberment: Crippled Children, Wounded Soldiers, and the Great War in Great Britain', *American Historical Review*, 99/4 (1994), 1167–1202; and Deborah Cohen, *The War Come Home: Disabled Veterans in Britain and Germany, 1914–1939* (Berkeley: University of California Press, 2001).

on disability-related issues and sparked an academic interest in disability history. For the general tenor of such tomes the following 1919 publication is of particular note: Arthur Keith's *Menders of the Maimed*—the title says it all, the heroic efforts of medical men in 'curing' the crippled.[5] The author stated: 'surgeons are being called on to restore movement to thousands of men who have been lamed or maimed in war'.[6] The decade of the 1920s saw the publication of the first dedicated volumes on disability history. Disability is therefore an integral part, directly or indirectly, of those who experienced the Great War.

Case studies of disabled characters in Tolkien's works

Tolkien's 'disabled' characters can be grouped into three categories, manifesting different types of disability:

- Realistic disability—with a tragic bent—in the figures of Sador (nicknamed Labadal = 'Hopafoot'), old servant to young Túrin, and Brandir, leader of the People of Haleth in the Forest of Brethil, who both appear in the tale of Túrin (in all its versions).
- Heroic disability, exemplified by Maedhros, eldest of the seven sons of Fëanor, and Beren 'One-Hand', significantly both figures from the equally heroic Silmarillion.
- Metaphysical disability, notably the character of Parish in *Leaf by Niggle*, and more controversially Frodo.

---

[5] Arthur Keith, *Menders of the Maimed: The Anatomical and Physiological Principles Underlying the Treatment of Injuries to Muscles, Nerves, Bones and Joints* (London: Hodder and Stoughton, 1919).
[6] *Ibid.*, p. vii.

Let us start with the two disabled characters in the tale of Túrin who form the narrative framework, in that one appears near the beginning, the other towards the end of the tale. Sador, the old servant in days of Túrin's childhood, is the counterpoint to Túrin at the beginning, while Brandir, also an older man, a lame village leader, is a counterpoint to Túrin's rash and impulsive actions near the end of the story. According to the social model of disability, these two would be the only genuinely disabled characters in Tolkien's texts, in that they neither lose their disability (as some others do, see below), nor overcome it, nor are seemingly unaffected by disability (in which case it is not actually disability).

Sador is the first of these characters we encounter, and also a figure dear to the young Túrin. Sador is described as

> a house-man in the service of Húrin; he was lame, and of small account. He had been a woodman, and by ill-luck or the mishandling of his axe he had hewn his right foot, and the footless leg had shrunken; and Túrin called him Labadal, which is 'Hopafoot', though the name did not displease Sador, for it was given in pity and not in scorn. (*UT*, p. 60)

As a child, Túrin seems caring and empathic towards Sador, unlike his mother Morwen, who describes Sador as 'self-maimed by his own want of skill, and he is slow with his tasks' (*UT*, p. 64). When Túrin has to leave home, he says to his mother 'But I shall leave you only with Sador, and blind Ragnir, and the old women' (*UF*, p. 71). This is the only mention of otherwise completely unknown Ragnir, and as far as I know the only mention of blindness in a real not metaphorical sense by Tolkien. Brandir is the main tragic figure because though

40

he tries his best, Túrin's catastrophic eruptions everywhere he goes prevents all the best intentions of Brandir. He

> was no man of war, being lamed by a leg broken in a misadventure in childhood; and he was moreover gentle in mood, loving wood rather than metal; and the knowledge of things that grow in the earth rather than other lore. (*UF*, p. 110)

As Glaurung the dragon draws nearer, a kinsman, one Hunthor, defends Brandir 'whose limbs by ill hazard cannot do as his heart would' (*UF*, p. 129). After Túrin, Níniel and the others have departed, Brandir girt himself 'with a short sword, as seldom before, and took his crutch, and went with what speed he might' limping after the others (*UF*, p. 132). So, as the tragedy unfolds, 'he cursed his fate and his weakness' (*UF*, p. 137). At the final confrontation Túrin calls him 'Club-foot': 'Would you slay us then with foul words, since you can wield no other weapon?' and also calls him a 'limping evil' (*UF*, p. 142). In the end, he is too late to prevent the deaths of Túrin or Niënor/Níniel simply because he is too slow, too disabled by the impairment of his lame leg. Both Sador and Brandir can be seen as convincing, realistic figures, whose impairments, brought about through no moral faults of their own but simply by accident, 'disable' them from helping Túrin and averting his doom.

Now a look at the 'heroic' figures, who both lose a hand yet transcend their impairment to the extent of being unaffected by their presumed disability. The first character who loses a hand is Maedhros, who was captured by Morgoth shortly after the Battle under the Stars (Dagor-nuin-Giliath), tortured and hung from the peak of Thangorodrim by his sword hand. He was rescued and freed by Fingon, son of Fingolfin, but to get him free of the shackles, his sword hand had to be chopped off. Maedhros subsequently learnt how to wield a sword in his remaining hand and 'lived to wield his sword with left hand more deadly than his right had been' (*Silmarillion*, p. 111). Maedhros is thus restored to his position as warrior and leader, much as Nuadha of the Silver Hand of Celtic Irish legend regains his position after losing a hand by having the eponymous silver prosthesis made. In fact, Maedhros becomes the mightiest in war of all the sons of Fëanor. This is part of the narrative of overcoming disability, of negating a disability—hence from this point of view, Maedhros's missing hand is not so much a real disability as a metaphor for a character defect that continues to haunt him. Fast-forward to the end of the First Age, when the seven sons of Fëanor are down to only two, Maedhros and Maglor, and still attempt to seize back the Silmarils. Maedhros succeeds in grasping one of the Silmarils, but it sears his hand, so that he throws himself clutching the Silmaril into an abyss.

> But the jewel burned the hand of Maedhros in pain unbearable; and he perceived that it was as Eönwë had said, and that his right thereto had become void, and that the oath was in vain. And being in anguish and despair he cast himself into a gaping chasm filled with fire, and so ended; and the Silmaril that he bore was taken into the bosom of the earth. (*Silmarillion*, pp. 253–54)

And similarly heroic is the case of apparent disability with Beren. The loss of his right hand is a kind of martyr's mark. In a way Beren even foreshadows 'the crippled and nine-fingered Frodo', something which Christine Chism claims is resonant of 'the costly ethics of renunciation, its willingness to question creativity to the point of disablement'.[7] The symbolic nature of Beren's loss of hand as a mark of martyrdom becomes even more apparent when one considers that in Tolkien's texts, Beren is the only (human) person to have been resurrected. 'None have ever come back from the mansions of the dead, save only Beren son of Barahir, whose hand had touched a Silmaril' (*Silmarillion*, pp. 104–05). Beren's tactile encounter with the Silmaril is permitted, and unlike other characters such as Maedhros who grasp a Silmaril, 'the jewel suffered his touch and hurt him not' (*Silmarillion*, p. 181). However, subsequently using the Silmaril as a kind of weapon against the hell-hound Carcharoth turns out to be a bad idea, since Beren 'thrust the Silmaril before the eyes of the wolf. But Carcharoth looked upon that holy jewel and was not daunted […] and gaping he took suddenly the hand within his jaws, and he bit it off at the wrist' (*Silmarillion*, p. 181). Beren survives the wound with its poison, and thereafter is named Erchamion (One-handed), 'and suffering was graven in his face' (*Silmarillion*, p. 183). When Beren goes to Thingol to present him with the promised Silmaril, he plays on the double meaning of the words 'Even now a Silmaril is in my hand', showing first his intact but empty left hand, and then the stump of his right arm (*Silmarillion*, p. 184). The story ends with an episode that has certain parallels with narratives surrounding medieval notions of sanctity and the appearance of the incorruptible corpse of the

---

[7] Christine Chism, 'Middle-earth, the Middle Ages, and the Aryan nation: Myth and history in World War II', in *Tolkien the Medievalist*, ed. by Jane Chance (London and New York: Routledge, 2003), pp. 63–92 (p. 88).

saint. When Carcharoth the hell-wolf is slain and the Silmaril finally retrieved, inside the half-consumed belly of the wolf 'the hand of Beren that held the jewel was yet incorrupt. But when Mablung reached forth to touch it, the hand was no more, and the Silmaril lay there unveiled' (*Silmarillion*, p. 186).

Beren and Maedhros may both be set in comparison with Nuadha of the Silver Hand, the Irish hero-deity who only regains his divine kingship once his lost hand is replaced with a silver prosthetic one, and he is thus no longer 'disabled' but made whole again, integer, or even said to possess idoneity, that is suitability for something—without the hand he is a maimed king, and thus not acceptable. Now interestingly there is a nice little link between Tolkien and Nuadha, via the Celtic god Nodens. Early on in his academic career (in 1932 to be precise), Tolkien famously wrote on the linguistics of the name Nodens for the archaeological report on the excavation at Lydney.[8] Situated on the steep banks of the River Severn in Gloucestershire, Lydney had a Romano-Celtic temple dedicated to Nodens, also known as Nodons or Nudens. Tolkien's linking of Nodens with Old Irish Núadu and Welsh Nudd has been accepted by later scholars. According to Nora Chadwick, Nodens 'may be identified with the Irish god Nuadu Argatlám, "Nuada of the silver hand". The name is known in Welsh tradition as Lludd Llaw Ereint ("Lludd of the silver hand")'.[9] The site at Lydney was not just a regular temple, but seemed

[8] J.R.R. Tolkien, 'The Name 'Nodens', in *Report on the Excavation of the Prehistoric, Roman, and Post-Roman Site in Lydney Park, Gloucestershire*, by R.E.M. Wheeler and T.V. Wheeler (London: Oxford University Press for the Society of the Antiquaries, 1932), pp. 132–37; reprinted in *Tolkien Studies*, 4 (2007), 177–83.

[9] Nora Chadwick, *The Celts* (London: Penguin, 1971), p. 167.

to have had a healing shrine function as well, with ancillary buildings such as a hostel for supplicants, a bath-house and 'an *abaton* or healing centre, where invalids were visited by the god or one of his sacred dogs of healing in their sleep.'[10] Tolkien had traced the name Nodens in other ancient languages and (perhaps hastily) concluded that the name signified either 'the catcher', 'the snarer', or 'the hunter'. Be that as it may, the connection between Nodens-Nuatha-Nudd, a maimed god, and a healing temple dedicated to him, will not have been lost on Tolkien, nor the further connection to his two heroically 'disabled' literary creations of Beren and Maedhros.

> Both Maedhros and Beren exhibit heroic disability in that both are large-than-life characters, who in their specific ways overcome their impairments. Applying the social model of disability here, I argue that Beren and Maedhros are temporarily impaired by each losing one of their hands, but never become disabled.

And finally let us turn to them more 'metaphysical' disabled figures. Beren's similarity with medieval notions of martyrdom has just been mentioned. Other characters also make for interesting comparisons with the medieval world which Tolkien knew so well. Parish, from *Leaf by Niggle*, 'had a lame leg, a genuine lame leg which gave him a good deal of Pain' (*PR*, p. 126). But Parish is only lame and demandingly needy, imposing on Niggle at the beginning of the story, while it is set in this world. From a medievalist perspective, he loses his limp gradually once re-united with Niggle in the Otherworld (Paradise?), where both are healed, the one of his lameness, the

---

[10] *Ibid.*

other of his 'niggling'. Over there, Parish still limped a little at first, but after time working together with Niggle, 'Parish lost his limp' (*Perilous Realm*, p. 139).

Tolkien's Otherworld in *Leaf by Niggle* echoes a concept according to which the medieval afterlife in heaven knew only of intact bodies. An interesting issue regarding medieval notions of disability more generally is what implication medieval notions of the afterlife had for the physically impaired. Medieval theologians and philosophers advocated a genuine corporal Resurrection, at which the body as well as the soul would enter the afterlife. The physical shape the bodies of the resurrected would have in heaven was that of perfect bodies, with no defects, therefore manifesting no conditions we would now term impairments. An exception might be the bodies of saints and martyrs, whose physical scars and deformities would still be present at the Resurrection, thereby setting them apart from the average impaired individual of this world. These notions of corporal resurrection with perfect bodies carry important consequences with them for medieval notions of what we would call identity and personhood, something that modern disability theorists have emphasised. By advocating resurrection with a perfect body, while at the same time body and soul were seen as closely linked, medieval notions of identity and/or personhood differed markedly from such modern theories with regard to physical impairment. In modern theories, physical impairment is seen to shape and influence an individual's identity, while in medieval thought, it appears, physical impairment was not regarded as a very important criterion for a person's identity. These complex medieval theological and philosophical ideas may be summed up as follows: everyone who goes to heaven is resurrected with a perfect body and at a perfect age (of around 30), and only the saints continue to bear the scars of their martyrdom as identifying marks of enhanced sanctity. In Paradise, there is no room for disability.

And then of course there is Frodo: Frodo is also like the medieval saints or martyrs, in that his disability remains with him even in Valinor/the Otherworld. That aside, Frodo is actually not particularly disabled: he has lost a finger, that is all, not even a thumb (which would affect physical ability much more). The disability seems to be far more something psychological, spiritual, or internal. With regard to Frodo's injuries, his wounds have left him permanently marked. Sam finds Frodo very pale on the second anniversary of the attack on Weathertop; 'I am wounded,' he answered, 'it will never heal' (*RK*, VI, ix). At the final good-bye at the Grey Havens, Frodo tells Sam: 'I have been too deeply hurt' (*RK*, VI, ix). The theme of martyrdom is even stronger earlier on in the story. After leaving Rivendell in 'Homeward Bound', Frodo complains of the pain in his shoulder from his wounding on Weathertop. Gandalf tries to console him, saying that some wounds 'cannot be wholly cured', but to that Frodo retorts:

'There is no real going back. Though I may come to the Shire, it will not seem the same; for I shall not be the same. I am wounded with knife, sting and tooth, and a long burden. Where shall I find rest?' (*RK*, VI, vii)

One may note here the trinity of wounds—literally a trinity as in a trebling, but also metaphorically a trinity that draws association with the Christian trinity. In his suffering for the bettering of Middle-earth, Frodo may be compared to the

47

medieval saints or martyrs, who equally suffered for a cause, so that perhaps Frodo's 'reward' is that his disability remains with him even in the Otherworld thus setting him apart from other mere mortals. It is tempting to think of Frodo as the martyr, the saint of Middle-earth.

This paper explored how disabled characters are used by Tolkien as tropes for a wider narrative purpose, which employs disability much as the 'narrative prosthesis' as suggested by literary critics Mitchell and Snyder.[11] They have argued that disability has been used as a device of characterisation in literature and film. While other marginalised identities have suffered cultural exclusion due to a dearth of images reflecting their experience, the marginality of disabled people has occurred in the midst of the perpetual circulation of images of disability in print and visual media. In this way, Tolkien has followed suit. He has, however, been far more nuanced and complex than the Mitchell-Snyder theory would allow for, in that instead of simply presenting one homogenous picture of disability as 'narrative prosthesis', Tolkien (informed by his knowledge of medieval and classical history and literature) has used disability in at least three different ways for three different kinds of literary figures: the realist, the heroic and the metaphysical.

---

[11] David T. Mitchell and Sharon L. Snyder, *Narrative Prosthesis: Disability and the Dependencies of Discourse* (Michigan: University of Michigan Press, 2001).

Works Consulted

Barnes, C., G. Mercer and T. Shakespeare, *Exploring Disability: A Sociological Introduction* (Cambridge: Polity Press, 1999)

Burke, Joanna, *Dismembering the Male: Men's Bodies, Britain and the Great War* (London: Reaktion, 1996)

Chadwick, Nora, *The Celts* (London: Penguin, 1971)

Chism, Christine, 'Middle-earth, the Middle Ages, and the Aryan nation: Myth and history in World War II', in *Tolkien the Medievalist,* ed. by Jane Chance (London and New York: Routledge, 2003), pp. 63–92

Cohen, Deborah, *The War Come Home: Disabled Veterans in Britain and Germany, 1914–1939* (Berkeley: University of California Press, 2001)

Keith, Arthur, *Menders of the Maimed: The Anatomical and Physiological Principles Underlying the Treatment of Injuries to Muscles, Nerves, Bones and Joints* (London: Hodder and Stoughton, 1919)

Koven, Seth, 'Remembering and Dismemberment: Crippled Children, Wounded Soldiers, and the Great War in Great Britain', *American Historical Review*, 99/4 (1994), 1167–1202

Metzler, Irina, *Disability in Medieval Europe* (London: Routledge, 2006)

Mitchell, David T., and Sharon L. Snyder, *Narrative Prosthesis: Disability and the Dependencies of Discourse* (Michigan: University of Michigan Press, 2001)

Risden, E.L., 'Middle-earth and the Waste Land: Greenwood, Apocalypse, and Post-War Resolution', in *Tolkien in the New Century: Essays in Honor of Tom Shippey*, ed. by John Wm. Houghton, Janet Brennan Croft, Nancy Martsch, John D. Rateliff and Robin Anne Reid (Jefferson: McFarland, 2014), pp. 57–64

Tolkien, J.R.R., 'The Name 'Nodens', in *Report on the Excavation of the Prehistoric, Roman, and Post-Roman Site in Lydney Park, Gloucestershire*, by R.E.M. Wheeler and T.V. Wheeler (London: Oxford University Press for the Society of the Antiquaries, 1932), pp. 132–37; reprinted in Tolkien Studies, 4 (2007), 177–83

Facing death: how characters in The Lord of the Rings meet the prospect of their own demise and the loss of others

Giovanni Carmine Costabile

Introduction

> It is hard to have patience with people who say 'There is no death' or 'Death doesn't matter'. There is death. And whatever is matters. And whatever happens has consequences, and it and they are irrevocable and irreversible. You might as well say birth doesn't matter.[1]

The present essay will focus on the different ways of facing death in *The Lord of the Rings*. Of course, there are as many ways of facing death as there are people. Nonetheless, I have endeavoured to identify all of those present in the Professor's masterpiece (and I hope I didn't miss anything!) and to classify them under twenty different labels based on two main categories that are in turn subdivided into three groups. In addition, within these groups there will be both negative and positive reactions. The main categories are:

A. Facing one's own death;
B. Facing the death of others.

Both of these could be split into two further groups:

---

[1] C.S. Lewis, *A Grief Observed* (London: Faber and Faber, 2013), p. 15.

A1. Facing the prospect of one's own death;
A2. Facing one's own actual death;
B1. Facing the prospect of the death of others;
B2. Facing the actual death of others.

Obviously, A2. makes no sense since facing one's own actual death means dying, and there are no ways to die other than just dying, at least from the point of view I am considering. There are indeed different ways of dying (slowly by bleeding or suffocation, instantly when the heart is pierced by an arrow or stabbed by a dagger etc.), but the passage that death represents is the same in all cases, and the way that that passage is confronted is what facing actual death means. Nevertheless, confronting death just means ceasing to exist, and there are no different ways of doing that. What, on the other hand, does make sense, and what matters, is the consideration of the different ways of facing a death that has still to occur, or the different ways of facing the death of others. Therefore, the above-mentioned groups can be reduced to A1. (which we can now simply call A.) and B1. and B2. Each of these will have at least two different subsections (for example, for A., we will have A.1 and A.2), referring respectively to the negative and positive reactions. Group B2. is an exception, since it has three subsections: B2.1 Negative reactions and B2.3 Positive reactions, but also B2.2 Ambiguous reactions. Having clarified these premises, I can now proceed with my investigation.

A. Facing one's own death

As Freud said, 'we cannot, indeed, imagine our own death', for 'whenever we try to do so we find that we survive ourselves as spectators'.[2] Even so, we can still imagine being someone else witnessing our death. What we absolutely cannot imagine is complete emptiness, which could even constitute a proof that something always has to exist, therefore death is not an absolute. Tolkien would surely have agreed on this matter. We only have to consider Letter 208: 'I become aware of the dominance [in *The Lord of the Rings*] of the theme of Death. [...] But certainly death is not an Enemy! I said, or meant to say, that the "message" was the hideous peril of confusing "true immortality" with limitless serial longevity. Freedom from time, and clinging to time. The *confusion* is the work of the Enemy, and one of the chief causes of human disaster. Compare the death of Aragorn with a Ringwraith. The elves call "death" the Gift of God (to Men)' (*Letters*, p. 267). I do not agree with Franco Manni when he says: 'Paradoxical! For Tolkien the "reward" is not a sort of "reawakening" followed by a sort of continuation of life, surrounded by light, celestial music and in the embrace of loved ones, as in popular phantasies of immortality, but is death ("true immortality")!'[3] I think the point here is the distinction between an immortality conceived as an eternal life on earth and an immortality taking place in heaven (or in Arda Healed!) instead. However, what does all that mean for our research, one may ask. Well, the fact is that the awareness of such a situation, or lack thereof, might inform

---

[2] Sigmund Freud, *Reflections on War and Death* (New York: Moffat, Yard & Company, 1918), p. 15.

[3] Franco Manni, 'A Eulogy of Finitude: Anthropology, Eschatology and Philosophy of History in Tolkien', in *The Broken Scythe: Death and Immortality in the Works of J.R.R. Tolkien*, ed. by Roberto Arduini and Claudio A. Testi (Zurich and Jena: Walking Tree Publishers, 2012), pp. 5–38 (p. 17).

the different reactions to the prospect of one's own death.

A.1 Negative reactions to the prospect of one's own death

As consequences of the lack of awareness of the fact that through death one may reach immortality, we find two different reactions that may be considered as childish: fear (though it may still be a reasonable reaction) and the unacceptable pre-emptive vengeance.

A.1 α *Pre-emptive vengeance*

Let's begin with the latter: what is pre-emptive vengeance? It is an act of vengeance which takes place before the action it is intended to avenge, where obviously the action is killing the would-be avenger. It is certainly not a coincidence that the above-mentioned subject is a vile Orc, Shagrat. 'Then he drew his sword. No doubt he meant to kill his captives, rather than allow them to escape or to be rescued; but it was his undoing' (*TT*, III, iii).

A.1 β *Fear*

Despite all their quarrelling and boasting attitudes, Orcs and the Mouth of Sauron are also prone to fear. For example, when Sam walked on the stairs of Cirith Ungol, 'the Orc crouched, and then with a hideous yelp of fear it turned and fled back as it had come' (*RK*, VI, i). But fear is something much more complex. As the story progresses, more and more occasions to be afraid emerge. The characters, however, especially the Hobbits, are growing much stronger and braver throughout the narrative and therefore are much more difficult to scare. In *The Fellowship of the Ring*, the Hobbits feel fear, and even terror, in the face of the Wicked Willow and, on many occasions (in the Shire, in Bree, at Weathertop, at the Ford, on the Anduin), of the Dark Riders. To be fair, I have to say that the Nazgûl inspire fear and terror through their supernatural influence in a way that not even the wight at the Barrow-downs can achieve. Furthermore, the rest of the fellowship, at least according to Legolas (*TT*, III, v), were also terrified by the apparition on the Great River. Fear is also what Frodo and Sam experience in the Dead Marshes. But, in *The Return of the King*, Merry ultimately takes part in the killing of the Witch King, displaying a courage even the bravest among men would envy (or celebrate). What a giant step from the timid Hobbit in *The Fellowship of the Ring*! Fear, of course, is a natural reaction, in some cases even a physical one: Frodo at Weathertop 'was quaking as if he was bitter cold' (*FR*, I, xi); upon feeling Grishnákh's breath on his cheeks, 'Pippin shuddered as hard cold fingers groped down his back' (*TT*, III, iii); while Sméagol, warned by Frodo not to betray his and Sam's trust if he did not want to find himself in danger, replies: 'Dreadful danger! Sméagol's bones shake to think of it' (*TT*, IV, iii). But fear may be overcome by courage, heroism, or even simple acceptance.

A.2 Positive reactions to facing the prospect of one's own death

This brings us to the positive reactions, that are exactly those I just mentioned. Acceptance paves the way for courage, that in and of itself sets the stage for heroism.

Acceptance of death may result from a clear-sighted understanding of what precisely death is. In Arda, people have a *fëa* and a *hröa*, which can be translated as soul and body, respectively. The *hröa* of the Elves cannot be separated from their *fëa*, except under exceptional circumstances, while the *fëa* of Men becomes separated from their hröa when death comes. This happens according to the nature of Men. Death, for Men (and Hobbits as well), is natural. Tolkien stated in his *Letters* that, according to the Elves, death is not 'the last enemy to be destroyed',[4] but 'the given nature of Men' (*Letters*, p. 285). And that is an awareness that could lead to its acceptance.

And in fact, acceptance of his death is what Bilbo exhibits at the very beginning of the book, in chapter I. A wise, serene, mature acceptance. Bilbo has read many elven books in Rivendell, and he therefore knows everything a Hobbit may possibly know about *fëar* and *hröar*. He knows what death is, and he accepts it. When he says to Gandalf: 'I feel I need a holiday, a very long holiday. […] Probably a permanent holiday: I don't expect I shall return. […] I am old, Gandalf. I don't look it, but I am beginning to feel it in my heart of hearts. […] Why, I feel all thin, sort of stretched, if you know what I mean: like butter that has been scraped over too much bread' (*FR*, I, i), what he actually means is that he needs to take a holiday and go to Rivendell. But the holiday is also a metaphor for death, for which he is prepared since he feels old and does not mean to return from his journey. The journey of no-return *par excellence* is, of course, death. This also recalls *Leaf by*

---

[4] I Corinthians 15. 26.

Niggle, whose protagonist has to prepare for a journey too, and the journey in the end turns out to be death. To be fair, Bilbo does not just want to die a good death, he also wishes to spend his last years well. In Lewis R. Aiken's words, 'acceptance of death's inevitability can be a disturbing, or at least sobering, experience and a source of great anxiety. However, it can also be a source of strength and motivation to make the most of whatever time one has left'.[5] Finally, in *The Return of the King*, Bilbo sets forth on his final journey: he is going to die in the Undying Lands, a (paradoxical) reward for being a Ringbearer.

Therefore, it is precisely the contrary of what Simone de Beauvoir says: whether you think of it as heavenly or as earthly, and in this case even if it is not yours, if you love life immortality *is* a consolation for death.[6] On the other hand, a subtler variant of acceptance is dignity. You simply cannot meet your own demise with dignity unless you have previously accepted it. Particularly dignified deaths are those of Denethor and Aragorn. But what are the conditions for a death to be described as having been faced with dignity? Let us ask Lars Sandman: 'If we […] look at how contingent dignity could be relevant for dying the good death, we can distinguish a number of different uses and meanings in the concept of dignity […]. First, we can have certain personal traits or character traits'.[7] Aragorn and Denethor both have these: they are both distinct, solemn, noble or, in the case of the former, even regal. 'Second,

---

[5] Lewis R. Aiken, *Dying, Death and Bereavement* (Mahwa, NJ: Lawrence Erlbaum Associate Publishers, 2001), p. 177.

[6] de Beauvoir's original statement can be found in: Simone de Beauvoir, *A Very Easy Death* (New York: Pantheon Books, 2013), p. 92.

[7] Lars Sandman, *A Good Death: On the Value of Death and Dying* (Maidenhead, Berkshire: Open University Press, 2005), p. 48.

we can have a certain social standing or role in society'.[8] Of course, they are, respectively, a king and a steward. 'Third, we can have a certain effect on other people—that we inspire awe or respect in them'.[9] This is precisely the effect that Denethor has in inspiring in Pippin the desire to be appointed as one of his guards, or Aragorn, to whom the others instinctively look for guidance. 'Fourth, we can have a certain way to relate to ourselves—in having self-respect or self-esteem'.[10] And I think this goes without saying for both Aragorn and Denethor. When Denethor dies, even Gandalf who is 'mad' at him for what he does (killing himself) and what he was trying to do (killing his son Faramir too), cannot help but implicitly recognize the dignity of his passing. He declares: 'So passes Denethor, son of Ecthelion' (*RK*, V, vii), where I think the mention of his father, for the sake of Gondor's strong appreciation of lineages, is meant to acknowledge some dignity even in the folly of his decision. In contrast, when Aragorn dies, there is no doubt it is a particularly dignified death, almost like that of a saint. 'Then a great beauty was revealed in him, so that all who after came looked on him in wonder; for they saw the grace of his youth, and the valour of his manhood, and the wisdom and majesty of his age were blended together. And long there he lay, an image of the splendour of the Kings of Men in glory undimmed before the breaking of the world' (*RK*, Appendix A, I, v). I will return to both Denethor and Aragorn later.

---

[8] *Ibid.*

[9] *Ibid.*

[10] *Ibid.*

A.2 β *Courage*

Now let us move on to courage, a possible outcome of acceptance. It can also have different sources. For example, when Frodo wakes up in the mound in the Barrow-downs, he feels that 'there is a seed of courage hidden (often deeply, it is true) in the heart of the fattest and most timid hobbit, waiting for some final and desperate danger to make it grow' (*FR*, I, viii). Aragorn at Helm's Deep is 'heedless of the darts of the enemy' (*TT*, III, vii), while when he finds the unconscious body of Frodo outside Shelob's lair, Sam cannot decide whether he is 'brave, or loyal, or filled with rage' (*TT*, IV, x). The bravest ones, however, probably those who find in themselves the courage to face the Witch King, who says to Gandalf: 'Do you not know Death when you see it?' (*RK*, V, iv). Gandalf 'did not move', even though the Witch King was about to strike him with his flaming sword. That indeed took much courage. Then something miraculous in its simplicity happens: 'a cock crowed' and 'as if in answer there came from far away another note. Horns, horns, horns. In dark Mindolluin's sides they dimly echoed. Great horns of the North wildly blowing. Rohan had come at last'. In Tom Shippey's words, 'the cockcrow itself is too laden with old significance to be just a motif. In a Christian society one cannot avoid the memory of the cock that crowed to Simon Peter as he denied Christ the third time. What did *that* cockcrow mean? Surely, that there was a Resurrection, that from now on Simon's despair and fear of death would be overcome'.[11] Also 'Tolkien too might think of

---

[11] T.A. Shippey, *The Road to Middle-earth: How J.R.R. Tolkien Created a New Mythology* (London: Harper Collins, 1990), p. 194.

the Norse legend of the "Undying Lands", the Odáinsakr: when king Hadding reached its boundaries, the witch who guided him killed a cock and threw it above the wall; a moment later he heard the cock crow, before he himself had to turn away and go back to mortality. Cockcrow means dawn, means day after night, life after death: it asserts a greater cycle above a lesser one'.[12] Simply put, the chain of thought proceeds as follows: as day follows night, so must life follow death; and that is a comforting thought, something that could have been given in answer to Callahan's statement: 'I want to find meaning in my death or, if not a full meaning, a way of reconciling myself to it. Some kind of sense must be made of my mortality'.[13] Or, as a dear friend of mine once put it, we have to ask ourselves what becomes of things such as life and death as soon as we start to think of them in terms of frame and picture. If death and life together form a picture, which one is the frame? Again, if the answer is immortality, we could not possibly agree more with the Professor, who, according to Shippey again, 'seems to be trying to persuade us to see death potentially as a gift or reward' because it leads to immortality.[14]

A.2 γ Heroism

And then, when we see things in such terms, we may feel bold and brave enough to perform the most heroic acts, as for example Boromir or Théoden do. It must be said, however, that their heroism may have a fatalist component, typical of

---

[12] *Ibid.*

[13] Daniel Callahan, *The Troubled Dream of Life: Living with Mortality* (New York: Georgetown University Press, 1993), p. 166.

[14] Shippey, p. 211.

Norse and Anglo-Saxon literature, something (to be banal) along the lines of: 'Everything is lost! I may as well do it!'. *The Homecoming of Beorhtnoth Beorthelm's Son* tells the story of the last battle of a group of Anglo-Saxon warriors led by Beorhtnoth against the Vikings, and the narrative tone is one of condemnation rather than appreciation. Shippey makes a similar observation when he says: 'Tolkien was himself a Christian and he faced a problem in the "theory of courage" he so much admired: its mainspring is despair, its spirit often heathen ferocity'.[15] However, what might be missed is the discriminating importance of the context. In the case of Boromir, not being heroic would mean losing the opportunity to save Merry and Pippin, and maybe Frodo, from captivity or death. There is altruism in his sacrifice, as Aragorn states: 'You have conquered. Few have won such a victory' (*TT*, III, i). In the case of Théoden, he would have died, as far as he knew, even if he had decided not to lead the final charge, he therefore wanted to take as many Orcs with him as he could. 'I will not end here, taken like an old badger in a trap. [...] I will bid men sound Helm's horn, and I will ride forth' (*TT*, III, vii). In both cases, this is not heroism for heroism's sake, as in the case of Beorhtnoth who allows the Vikings to cross the crucial bridge which could have been easily defended by just a handful of soldiers, suffering negligible losses while inflicting heavy damage to his opponents. Sacrifice of position, in this case, means sacrificing one's own life. And what for? Although the actions (sacrificing one's life, or being prepared to do so), and also the outcome (death), at least in Boromir's case, may be similar, the sense is very different, and this is what

---

[15] *Ibid.*, p. 140.

we should highlight. To Boromir I would also like to dedicate de Beauvoir's saying: 'the absolute can be enclosed within the last moments of a dying person'.[16] 'But Boromir did not speak again' (*TT*, III, i).

B. Facing the death of others

As stated above, the topic of facing the death of others is also two-fold. In fact, it is twice two-fold, since we can have both negative and positive reactions both to the prospect of the death of others and to their actual death (although in the case of B3., as indicated in my introduction above, we can also have ambiguous reactions). Such duplicity is well expressed by Zygmunt Bauman: 'The death of others may be a benchmark for my own survival success, but it is the life of others which made that success desirable in the first place, as well as making it now worthy of effort'.[17] We will see how in the reactions both to the prospect of death and to the actual death of others these two instances come into play.

B1. Facing the prospect of the death of others

One of the possible reactions to the prospect of the death of others is the same as another we met when confronting one's own death: I am referring to heroism, which of course figures among the positive reactions. The other positive reactions are: concern, altruism, sacrifice and healing. Instead I could find only one negative reaction, with which I will begin: suicide.

[16] de Beauvoir, p. 63.

[17] Zygmunt Bauman, *Immortality and Other Life Strategies* (Cambridge: Polity Press, 1992), p. 37.

B1.1 Negative reactions to facing the prospect of the death of others

B1.1 α Suicide

Of course, I am about to discuss Denethor's suicide. To make it even worse, it is a suicide which was meant to take the life of Denethor's son Faramir too. 'Why should we not go to death side by side?' (*RK*, V, vii) the steward asks Gandalf. And, when Faramir said: 'So be it!' in answer to Denethor's statement that 'in desperate hours gentleness may be repaid with death', Denethor's reply was: 'But not with your death only, Lord Faramir: with the death also of your father, and of all of your people' (*RK*, V, iv). It is true that in this last passage Denethor had not decided yet on suicide and the murder of his son, but it is by following the course of such thoughts that he finally arrives at his final decision. 'Better to burn sooner than late, for burn we must. Go back to your bonfire! And I? I will go now to my pyre. To my pyre! No tomb for Denethor and Faramir. No tomb! No long slow sleep of death embalmed. We will burn like heathen kings before ever a ship sailed hither from the West. The West has failed. Go back and burn!' (*RK*, V, iv). Weisman and Hackett have written that 'an appropriate death must satisfy four principal requirements: (1) conflict is reduced; (2) compatibility with the ego ideal is achieved; (3) continuity of important relations is preserved or restored; (4) consummation of a wish is brought about'.[18] I think it appears clear that in his madness Denethor feels that the death he seeks

[18] A.D. Weisman and T.P. Hackett, 'Predilection to death. Death and dying as a psychiatric problem', *Psychosomatic Medicine*, 23 (1961), 232–56 (p. 248).

would satisfy all of these four requirements: conflict is reduced since he and his son would escape the present situation of war, in the siege of Minas Tirith; compatibility with the ego ideal is achieved in dying like the kings of old; continuity of relations is preserved or restored, in his mind at least, since he is going to take his son Faramir with him as well; the consummation of a wish, to be obeyed and to die as he wishes, is brought about.

But let us consider Faramir. When Pippin goes to see him, before Denethor orders him to be taken to the crypts in Rath Dínen, he 'lay upon his bed [...] dying someone said' (*RK*, V, v). The keywords are 'someone said', since he is not actually dying, as Gandalf knows, and that is the main reason why he abandons Théoden to his fate and goes instead to rescue Faramir. But there is a link between lying in bed and dying that is deeply ingrained in our minds. As Philippe Ariés pointed out, 'one awaited death lying down, *gisant*'.[19] A typical expression he quotes is '*gisant au lit malade*, lying on my sickbed'.[20] In this case the illness may be cured, but that doesn't mean it isn't a sickbed. There Faramir, paraphrasing what de Beauvoir says about her mother: 'rested and dreamed, infinitely far removed from his rotting flesh, his ears filled with the sound of Denethor's lies; his whole person was concentrated upon one passionate hope—getting well'.[21] But for that to be accomplished, he has to wait for the return of the king.

---

[19] Philippe Ariés, *Western Attitudes Towards Death: From the Middle Ages to the Present* (London: The John Hopkins University Press, 1994), p. 8.
[20] *Ibid.*
[21] de Beauvoir, p. 77.

B1.2 Positive reactions to facing the prospect of the death of others

B1.2 α Concern

Although all the members of the fellowship could be said to be constantly concerned about the well-being of other members, for reasons of brevity I will focus on Aragorn and Gandalf and on two occasions. 'Which way did he go? Was Frodo here?' (*TT*, III, i) Aragorn asks the dying Boromir. He is worried about Frodo, and of course in his being worried there is a component of concern about a possible retrieval of the Ring by the Enemy, but there is also genuine human concern about the fate of a friend. The same can be said of Gandalf in Minas Tirith. 'When will Faramir return?' (*RK*, V, i), he asks. Certainly, he wants to speak with him, but also in this case I think there is a sincere concern for the well-being of an ally.

B1.2 β Altruism

Altruism may be defined as the availability to put others before oneself. Proof of this attitude is given by Aragorn, who pledges his life and death to Frodo (*FR*, I, x), and Legolas who, when Éomer threatens to kill his friend Gimli, says: 'You would die before your stroke fell' (*TT*, III, ii), thus putting his own life to risk. Also Merry and Pippin, in swearing to serve Théoden and Denethor respectively, are willing to put their own lives at stake for the good of others.

B1.2 γ Heroism

We have already analysed heroism under the A. category, but that heroism mainly consisted in being brave enough to face one's own death. Here instead we are going to consider a heroism that results from having to face the prospect of death of someone else, in this case that of Théoden. The heroine is Éowyn, who reacts with a sudden surge of resolve and determination when the king of Rohan is injured and falls from his saddle to the ground. She will face the Witch King who, as we have seen, claims to be Death itself. 'Come not between the Nazgûl and his prey! Or he will not slay thee in thy turn. He will bear thee away to the houses of lamentation, beyond all darkness, where thy flesh shall be devoured, and thy shrivelled mind be left naked to the Lidless Eye' (*RK*, V, vi). But Éowyn has had enough: 'Do what you will; but I will hinder it' she says, resolute. The Nazgûl answers quoting an ancient prophecy: 'Hinder me? Thou fool. No living man may hinder me!' Éowyn's reply could not be more powerful: 'But no living man am I! You look upon a woman. Éowyn I am, Éomund's daughter. You stand between me and my lord and kin. Begone, if you be not deathless! For living or dark undead, I will smite you, if you touch him'. And indeed she keeps her word: 'With her last strength she drove her sword between crown and mantle, as the great shoulders bowed before her. The sword broke sparkling into many shards. The crown rolled away with a clang. Éowyn fell forward upon her fallen foe. But lo! the mantle and hauberk were empty. Shapeless they lay now on the ground, torn and tumbled; and a cry went up into the shuddering air, and faded to a shrill wailing, passing with the wind, a voice bodiless and thin that died, and was swallowed up, and was never heard again in that age of the world'. Thus ends the Witch King. But Théoden, Éowyn's kin, is slain. 'My body is broken. I go to my fathers' he says, echoing a literary topos of the Middle Ages, that of the premonition of death. As Ariés tells us, medieval characters simply cannot die 'without having had time to realize they were going to die'.[22] The motive is truly widespread. In *The Song of Roland* we learn that Roland at Roncesvaux 'feels that death holds him fast, for it has travelled from his head to his heart'. He 'feels that the end of his time has come'.[23] Tristan, in *The Romance of Tristan and Iseult*, 'knew that his life was going, and that he must die'.[24] Morgan's paramour in Malory's *Le Morte d'Arthur* says: 'deep draughts of death draw to my heart that I may not live',[25] while the dying Gawain writes a letter to Lancelot 'and at the date of this letter was written, but two hours and a half afore my death'.[26] But 'let us note that the warning came through natural signs or, even more frequently, through an inner conviction rather than through a supernatural, magical premonition'.[27]

---

[22] Ariés, pp. 2–3.

[23] 'The Song of Roland', trans. by Jessie Crosland, *In Parentheses* (Cambridge, Ontario: In parentheses Publications, 1999), 174–75, pp. 34–35 <http://www.yorku.ca/inpar/roland_crosland.pdf> [accessed 2 October 2016].

[24] *The Romance of Tristan and Iseult*, ed. by J. Bédier, trans. by H. Belloc (London: George Allen & Company, 1913), p. 170.

[25] Thomas Malory, *Le Morte d'Arthur* (Hazleton, Pennsylvania: The Electronic Classics Series Publication, 2012), p. 523.

[26] *Ibid.*, p. 440.

[27] Ariés, p. 4.

Gandalf knows death is not final. He is a Maia, an angelic being. But that does not make his sacrifice any easier, nor any less admirable. He is giving his life for the sake of others, against a formidable enemy: nothing less than a Balrog, a demon of old, a servant of Morgoth, born of flame and shadow. He does not yet know he will rise from the dead as The White Wizard. All he knows is that his sacrifice may give Frodo and the others a chance to escape from Moria, and he willingly decides to submit to it. '"Fly, you fools!" he cried, and he was gone' (*FR*, II, v). Even his last thought is for the safety of others, even in his final moment before falling into the abyss he pronounces words of heart-felt concern for others. If he sounds rude in calling them 'fools', it is because he wants to communicate the urgent need for them to flee, he has to arouse them from their state of passive spectatorship for them to realize they have to go. Directing one's last words to the well-being of others is a gesture that even history's most renowned and willing sacrificial victim, Jesus Christ, does not share. His last words, 'It is finished',[28] are instead of concern for himself: 'now I've done what I had to, I'm free to go' is what they mean. I am not the first to suggest a comparison between Gandalf and Christ. For example, Verlyn Flieger talks about the 'sum of [...] evidence' that 'points persuasively to an interpretation of Gandalf as a kind of Christ. He is a being of light, associated with, or comparable to a god; he is aware of his end before it happens, and accepts it; he dies, is resurrected, transformed, appears to his followers on the road (in this case

---

[28] John 19. 30.

Fangorn Forest), and at the end of the book, leaves bodily for the Undying Lands'.[29]

B1.2 ε *Healing*

Another way of dealing with the prospect of the death of others is to intervene actively to prevent it. I am not talking about intervening against those who mean harm to them, but about coming to the aid of others. I am talking about healing. The first example of healing in *The Lord of the Rings* is that of Frodo's wound inflicted by the Witch King at Weathertop. It is first treated by Aragorn before being finally cured by Elrond. But Aragorn's most important task of healing is the healing of Faramir and Éowyn in the Houses of Healing in Minas Tirith. 'Life to the dying in the king's hands lying' (*RK*, V, viii) they say, before he heals Faramir. The ability to heal reveals Aragorn as the legitimate heir to the throne of Gondor because, as Ioreth says: 'The hands of the king are the hands of a healer'. 'Awake, Éowyn' is all he needs to say for her to wake up from her deadly slumber. It is evident that Aragorn is also something of a Christ-like figure; Shippey, referring to a different episode, points it out,[30] though in the present case the comparison is obvious since the episode cannot fail to recall the evangelical: 'Lazarus, come forth'.[31] Healing is, of course, borne of altruism and concern for the health of others, and it can also be said, in some sense, to be a form of heroism.

---

[29] Verlyn Flieger, *Green Suns and Faërie: Essays on J.R.R. Tolkien* (Kent, Ohio: The Kent State University Press, 2012), p. 227.

[30] Shippey, p. 181.

[31] John 11. 43.

B.2 Facing the actual death of others

In the case of facing the actual death of others too, we were only able to find one reaction which is clearly negative: acting cruelly towards a dying/dead body. In addition we have two ambiguous reactions: playing a game and celebrating with joy. Both would appear to be positive in their content (a game and joy), but, even if the dead are enemies, it does not seem entirely fair from a moral standpoint to act in this way in the face of the death of others. I would also include in this a sub-section responding to the death of others, since Saruman does this in an elusive way that is typical of him. Then there are the positive reactions: celebrating a funeral, disposing of the bodies, being overcome with rage and grief-stricken mourning. These are positive both in respect to the action themselves (even rage and grief may be just when they are righteous) and to their motivations.

B2.1 Negative reactions to facing the actual death of others

B2.1 α *Acting cruelly towards a dying/dead body*

Acting cruelly towards a dying/dead body is an infamous act, and in fact it is performed by a vile Orc, Shagrat. "'Got you, Gorbag" he cried. "Not quite dead, eh? Well, I'll finish my job now'" (*RK*, VI, i). Very Orcish.

B2.2 Ambiguous reactions to facing the actual death of others

B2.2 α *Playing a game*

By 'playing a game', I am referring to Gimli and Legolas's account of their killing of Orcs. '"Two!" said Gimli' (*TT*, III, vii) and the game began. Then '"Twenty-one!" cried Gimli [...]. "Now my count surpasses Master Legolas again"'. In the end the count gets to '"Forty-two, Master Legolas!"' (*TT*, III, viii) and the Elf admits it surpasses his own by one. Now, even admitting those killed are evil Orcs, how do we judge such a reaction? Probably we should take into account the stress of war. Seeing your friends hurt or dying could require some kind of distraction to reduce the tension. Finding oneself on the wrong side of a siege is never easy, as in the case of the trench warfare Tolkien himself had to endure. He fought the battle of the Somme and lost two dear friends and fellow members of the Tea Club Barrovian Society, Rob Gilson and G.B. Smith, in that terrible war.[32]

---

[32] From Humphrey Carpenter, *J.R.R. Tolkien: A Biography* (London: Harper Collins, 2002), pp. 118–21: 'Tolkien never forgot what he called the "animal horror" of trench warfare'; upon learning the news of Gilson's death, 'Tolkien wrote to Smith: "I do not feel a member of a complete body now"'; Smith himself, not long before dying, had written to Tolkien: 'My chief consolation if I am scuppered tonight [...] there will still be left a member of the great T.C.B.S. to voice what I dreamed and we all agreed upon. [...] Death can make us loathsome and helpless as individuals, but it cannot put an end to the immortal four! [...] May God bless you, John Ronald, and may you say the things I have tried to say long after I am not there to say them, if such be my lot'. From John Garth, *Tolkien and the Great War: The Threshold of Middle-earth* (London: Harper Collins, 2004), pp. 296, 265: 'Although the

B2.2 β Celebrating with joy

When the Ring is destroyed and Sauron's dominion ends, all the members of the fellowship celebrate the happening with great joy. 'A great shadow has departed' (*RK*, VI, iv) says Gandalf with a large smile, before laughing heartily. All the people in Minas Tirith sing the Song of the Eagle: 'Sing now, ye people of the Tower of Anor, for the Realm of Sauron is ended for ever, and the Dark Tower is thrown down' (*RK*, VI, v). Here, too, Sauron's death is met with an attitude which seems inconsistent with the seriousness and gravity it would theoretically call for. But we have to take into account that it is a tyrant's death, the Dark Lord's death, and therefore there are plenty of reasons to rejoice, as the Eagle sings.

B2.2 γ Responding to the death of others

As I was saying earlier, Saruman's response to the death of the Rohirrim is not a real act of responsibility, since he claims it is not his fault if brave riders have met their end in war. His argument is not without its pitfalls: 'But my lord of Rohan, am I to be called a murderer, because valiant men have fallen in battle? If you go to war, needlessly, for I did not desire it, men will be slain. But if I am a murderer on that account, then

---

stereotypical picture of the Western Front does not include soldiers reading the Mabinogion with its Welsh Arthuriana, as G.B. Smith did, or William Morris's *The Earthly Paradise*, which Tolkien carried, in fact quest literature was profoundly popular'; 'Rob Gilson, hearing a nightingale in the early hours one May morning from his trench dugout, thought it "wonderful that shells and bullets shouldn't have banished them, when they are always so shy of everything human"'.

all the House of Eorl is stained with murder; for they have fought many wars, and assailed those who defied them' (*TT*, III, x). The argument is fallacious, since Rohan was left with no choice but to go to war, and that was Saruman's responsibility, since he commanded the Orcs to assail men.

B2.3 Positive reactions to facing the actual death of others

B2.3 α *Celebrating a funeral*

The most famous funeral in *The Lord of the Rings* takes place after Boromir's death. His body is put on a boat and released to the currents of the Great River. Quoting Pat Reynolds, 'With the image of death-as-journey it is not surprising that boats are an important component in many forms of the funeral in the prehistoric north. Boat-pyres, funeral barges, boats inside barrows and boat-shaped grave markers abound. The ship as a symbol can be traced back to the earliest times: it was one of the symbols of the fertility god Freyr, and seems to be more associated with the old gods, the Vanir, than with the new gods, the Æsir'.[33] A link between the themes of death (and rebirth) and fertility can be traced as far back as the Ancient Egyptians, who associated both of these themes with the colours black and green.[34] So, as we were saying, Boromir is carried away

---

[33] Pat Reynolds, 'Death and Funerary Practices in Middle-earth', The Tolkien Society <https://www.tolkiensociety.org/wp-content/uploads/2016/11/Death-and-funerary-practices-in-Middle-earth.pdf> [accessed 5 October 2017].

[34] From April McDevitt, 'Color (iwen)', *Ancient Egypt: The Mythology* <http://www.egyptianmyths.net/colors.htm> [accessed 2 October 2016]. Black: 'In ancient Egypt, black (kem) was a symbol of death and of the night.

by the river. But not before Aragorn and Legolas have sung a song to commemorate him: 'What news from the West, O wandering wind, do you bring to me tonight? Have you seen Boromir the Tall by moon or by starlight?' (*TT*, III, i). A song of commemoration is also sung by Frodo in Lórien in Gandalf's memory, an occasion which is also a sort of funeral:

> He stood upon the bridge alone
> And Fire and Shadow both defied
> His staff was broken on the stone
> In Khazad-dûm his wisdom died (*FR*, II, vii)

Bauman says that 'commemorative rites rehearse the non-

Osiris, the king of the afterlife was called "'the black one." One of the few real-life people to be deified, Queen Ahmose-Nefertari was the patroness of the necropolis. She was usually portrayed with black skin, although she was not a negro. Anubis, the god of embalming was shown as a black jackal or dog, even though real jackals and dogs are typically brown. As black symbolized death it was also a natural symbol of the underworld and so also of resurrection. Unexpectedly perhaps, it could also be symbolic of fertility and even life! The association with life and fertility is likely due to the abundance provided by the dark, black silt of the annually flooding Nile. The color of the silt became emblematic of Egypt itself and the country was called "kemet" (the Black Land) by its people from early antiquity'.
Green: 'The color green (*wadj*) was the color of vegetation and new life. To do "green things" was slang for beneficial, life-producing behavior. As mentioned above, Osiris was often portrayed with green skin and was also referred to as "the Great Green". Green malachite was a symbol of joy and the land of the blessed dead was described as the "field of malachite." In Chapter 77 of the Book of the Dead, it is said that the deceased will become a falcon "whose wings are of green stone". Highly impractical of course, it is obvious that the color of new life and re-birth is what is important. The Eye of Horus amulet was commonly made of green stone as well'.

finality of death. They also represent the continuing existence of community as the pledge to overcome, at least for a time, the individual transience. They separate the moment of bodily death from that of social death, making the second independent of the other and endowing only the second, social, death with the status of finality. While giving form to the dream of immortality, they deploy the dread of mortality in the service of communal cohesion'.[35] In the above-mentioned cases, however, this may not seem to be necessarily so. One could say that the cohesion of the fellowship is not reinforced by the commemoration of Gandalf's death, since the fellowship is split a few weeks after that event. We could say rather that the fellowship is disbanded *because* of Gandalf's absence. But that would miss the fundamental point: the relation which the 'funeral' reinforces is not that among the members of the fellowship in its entirety, but only between two very particular members: Frodo and Sam, who discuss the song and later on set forth, just the two of them, on their way to Mordor to destroy the Ring. Theirs is the most important task, and if they are successful it is, possibly, in part because their friendship has been improved by their sharing of that grief. Possibly. In Boromir's case as well, it seems that his funeral really helps to establish a strong bond of friendship between Aragorn, Gimli and Legolas, who thereafter never separate until the Ranger is appointed as King in Gondor.

B2.3 β *Disposing of the body*

There are many ways of disposing of a dead body. As we have

---

[35] Bauman, pp. 52–53.

seen, Boromir was left to the streams of the Great River, which recalls the Viking custom in funerary rites, while Denethor burned in the flames and was incinerated like the kings of old. But the most common way of disposing of a body is, of course, by burying it. As Ariés reminds us with regards to this subject, 'the world of the living had to be kept separated from that of the dead. In Rome, the law of the Twelve Tables forbad burial *in urbe*, within the city. The Theodosian Code repeated the same interdict, so that the *sanctitas* of the inhabitants' homes would be preserved.[36] Now, while the Barrow-downs may be included within such a rule, having been built far away from the nearest town, the same cannot be said of Rath Dínen in Minas Tirith. It is there that Denethor goes to die, 'between pale domes and empty halls and images of men long dead' (*RK*, V, iv). The people of Gondor were obsessed by death, so much so that 'kings made tombs more splendid than houses of the living, and counted old names in the rolls of their descent dearer than the names of sons' (*TT*, IV, v).

B2.3 γ *Being overcome with rage*

Sam is overcome with rage when he finds what he thinks to be the dead body of Frodo, fights Shelob and even goes so far as to stab her (*TT*, IV, x). Furthermore, when he finds out that his master is not dead, he feels anger, in part directed towards himself, since it was he who abandoned Frodo to the Orcs. He then climbs the steps of Cirith Ungol, shouting to the Orc he meets: 'Just show me the way up, or I'll skin you!' (*RK*, VI, i). Rage is generally not considered very positively, but in

---

[36] Ariés, p. 15.

this context, it is clearly positive, allowing Sam to rescue his master Frodo from captivity and whatever devilry the Orcs had in store for him.

B2.3 δ *Grief-stricken mourning*

Freud talks about 'our complete collapse at the death of a person closely related to us, such as a parent, a wife or husband, a brother or sister, a child or a dear friend. We bury our hopes, our wishes and our desires with the dead; we are inconsolable and refuse to replace our loss'.[37] And also de Beauvoir states that: 'when someone you love dies you pay the sin of outliving her with a thousand piercing regrets'.[38] Tolkien knew very well what that means, since he experienced the loss of his parents at a very young age. Humphrey Carpenter talks at length about the author's terrible experience of losing his mother, whose only consolation was the Christian faith she herself had and had taught him.[39] It was a life-changing experience. In fact, even many years later, in 1965, he writes: 'When I think of my

[37] Freud, p. 16.

[38] de Beauvoir, p. 94.

[39] From Carpenter, pp. 50–51: '"My own dear mother was a martyr indeed, and it is not to everybody that God grants so easy a way to his great gifts as he did to Hilary and myself, giving us a mother who killed herself with labour and trouble to ensure us keeping the faith". Ronald Tolkien wrote this nine years after his mother's death. […] Certainly the loss of his mother had a profound effect on his personality. […] He was by nature a cheerful almost irrepressible person with a great zest for life. He loved good talk and physical activity. […] But from now onwards there was to be a second side […]. This side of him was capable of bouts of profound despair. More precisely, and more closely related to his mother's death, when he was in this mood he had a deep sense of impending loss. Nothing was safe. Nothing would last. No battle would be won forever'.

mother's death [...] worn out with persecution, poverty, and, largely consequent, disease, in the effort to hand on to us small boys the Faith, [...] I find it very hard and bitter, when my children stray away [from the Church]' (*Letters*, pp. 353–54). Tolkien also wrote very touching words concerning his friend C.S. Lewis's demise: 'So far I have felt [...] like an old tree that is losing all its leaves one by one: this feels like an axe-blow near the roots' (*Letters*, p. 341). Words that could have been pronounced by Faramir or Denethor after they have learnt of the death of Boromir, the valiant brother and son, respectively. Faramir says that upon learning this news 'my heart was filled with grief and pity' (*TT*, IV, v), proof it is not a work of the enemy for him to learn that, since the Enemy's works instead fill hearts with loathing. Also Denethor cries in despair: 'My Boromir!' (*RK*, V, i).

But the saddest grief is Arwen's for Aragorn. It was so powerful that all she could do was to go 'forth from the House, and the light of her eyes was quenched, and it seemed to her people that she had become cold and grey as nightfall in winter that comes without a star' (*RK*, Appendix A, I, v). She could perhaps be comforted by Lewis's words: 'And then one or other dies. And we think of this as love cut short; like a dance stopped in mid career or a flower with its head unluckily snapped off—something truncated and therefore, lacking its due shape. I wonder. If, as I can't help suspecting, the dead also feel the pains of separation, [...] then [...] bereavement is a universal and integral part of our experience of love. [...] It is not a truncation of the process, but one of its phases; not the interruption of the dance, but the next figure. We are "taken out of ourselves" by the loved one while she is here. Then comes the tragic figure of the dance in which we must learn to be still taken out of ourselves though the bodily presence is withdrawn, to love the very Her, and not fall back to loving our past, or our memory, or our sorrow, or our relief from sorrow, or our own love.'[40] But she is not comforted. Nor would she accept the idea of the Italian poet Petrarch, according to whom, in the words of Bernhard Jussen and Ramie Targoff, 'only death enables love […] to manifest itself in the core of its essence'.[41] So she 'laid herself to rest upon Cerin Amroth; and there is her green grave, until the world is changed, and all the days of her life are utterly forgotten by men that come after, and elanor and niphredil bloom no more east of the sun' (*RK*, App. A, I, v). And, if Aragorn and Arwen could be said to re-enact Beren and Lúthien's story, and Tolkien saw himself as Beren and his wife Edith as his Lúthien, then it follows that Aragorn and Arwen could also represent, in a sense, the Professor and Edith. 'But now she has gone before Beren, leaving him indeed one-handed, but he has no power to move the inexorable Mandos, and there is no *Dor Gyrth i chuinar*, the Land of the Dead that Live, in this Fallen Kingdom of Arda, where the servants of Morgoth are worshipped' (*Letters*, p. 417).

Conclusions

We have examined both reactions to one's own death and to the death of others, in the latter case regarding the prospect of the death of others and their actual death. We have seen

---

[40] Lewis, pp. 43–44.

[41] Bernhard Jussen and Ramie Targoff, 'Introduction: Love after Death. A Sketch', in *Love after Death: Conceptions of Posthumous Love in Medieval and Early Modern Culture*, ed. by Bernhard Jussen and Ramie Targoff (Berlin: De Gruyter, 2015), pp. 3–16 (p. 15).

there can be both negative and positive (or even ambiguous) reactions, and how each of these is represented in *The Lord of the Rings* and how it can be assessed. To conclude, I would like to quote another passage from de Beauvoir's *A Very Easy Death*, a passage which Tolkien himself in an interview of 1968[42] said held the deepest meaning of *The Lord of the Rings*: 'There is no such thing as a natural death: nothing that happens to a man is ever natural, since his presence calls the world into question. All men must die: but for every man his death is an accident, and even if he knows it and consents to it, an unjustifiable violation'[43] To explain this passage, it is probably appropriate to consider what Lorenzo Gammarelli says: 'Bereavement is a fundamental concept in Tolkien's works, both longer and shorter. Bereavement is the sense of loss, the feeling or atmosphere that dominates all the stories, particularly those where Elves are involved. It is, however, also a direct consequence of death: sadness and anxiety for the loss of someone dear who is no more. The same feeling, or one much alike, is noted when we come into realms outside normal reality, such as the land of the Elves. Upon returning into our mundane world, we are confronted with a lack of comprehension by all those people who have not shared our experience. Bereavement, therefore, is the link between the sensations we feel when we confront death and the sensations one feels when returning from Faëry. It is a bridge between death and immortality'.[44] And this is true especially in Frodo's case, who upon his return to the Shire definitely feels a sense of

---

[42] *Tolkien in Oxford*, dir. by Leslie Megahey (BBC, 1968).

[43] de Beauvoir, p. 106.

[44] Lorenzo Gammarelli, 'On the Edge of the Perilous Realm', in Arduini and Testi, pp. 103–16 (p. 114).

bereavement which he expresses in the poem attributed to him, 'The Sea-Bell'. Regarding this poem, Shippey says that 'Frodo doubted his own salvation. This may be seen as a dark illusion born of losing the "addictive" Ring, but one senses that Tolkien was doubtful too: not of salvation, but of the legitimacy of his own mental wanderings. [...] It is hard not to think that by then he saw himself (perhaps only at times) as Fíriel, Farmer Maggot, Frodo, "" and eventually Smith—a mortal deserted by the immortals and barred from their company. He no longer imagined himself re-joining his own creations after death, like Niggle; he felt they were lost, like the Silmarils'.[45] And Flieger states that for Tolkien 'hope and desire seem to be always balanced by despair, so that this final vision [that Frodo has on the boat to Aman] remains a vision only, called into question by his hard-won knowledge of the dark, given affirmation by his continuing faith in the light'.[46] But I would like to leave the last words to Tolkien himself: 'It is one of the mysteries of pain that it is, for the sufferer, an opportunity for good, a path of ascent however hard. But it remains an "evil"' (*Letters*, p. 126).

---

[45] Shippey, pp. 250–51.

[46] Verlyn Flieger, *Splintered Light: Logos and Language in Tolkien's World* (Kent, Ohio: The Kent State University Press, 2002), p. 165.

Works Consulted

Aiken, Lewis R., *Dying, Death and Bereavement* (Mahwa, New Jersey: Lawrence Erlbaum Associate, Publishers, 2001)

Ariés, Philippe, *Western Attitudes Towards Death: From the Middle Ages to the Present* (London: The John Hopkins University Press, 1994)

Bauman, Zygmunt, *Mortality, Immortality and Other Life Strategies* (Cambridge: Polity Press, 1992)

Callahan, Daniel, *The Troubled Dream of Life: Living with Mortality* (New York: Georgetown University Press, 1993)

Carpenter, Humphrey, *J.R.R. Tolkien: A Biography* (London: Harper Collins, 2002)

de Beauvoir, Simone, *A Very Easy Death* (New York: Pantheon Books, 2013)

Flieger, Verlyn, *Splintered Light: Logos and Language in Tolkien's World* (Kent, Ohio: The Kent State University Press, 2002)

——, *Green Suns and Faërie: Essays on J.R.R. Tolkien* (Kent, Ohio: The Kent State University Press, 2012)

Freud, Sigmund, *Reflections on War and Death* (New York: Moffat, Yard & Company, 1918)

Gammarelli, Lorenzo, 'On the Edge of the Perilous Realm', in *The Broken Scythe: Death and Immortality in the Works of J.R.R. Tolkien*, ed. by Roberto Arduini and Claudio A. Testi (Zurich and Jena: Walking Tree Publishers, 2012), pp. 103–16

Garth, John, *Tolkien and the Great War: The Threshold of Middle-earth* (London: Harper Collins, 2004)

Jussen, Bernhard, and Ramie Targoff, 'Introduction: Love after Death. A Sketch', in *Love after Death: Conceptions of Posthumous Love in Medieval and Early Modern Culture*, ed. by Bernhard Jussen and Ramie Targoff (Berlin: De Gruyter, 2015), pp. 3–16

Lewis, C.S., *A Grief Observed* (London: Faber and Faber, 2013)

Malory, Thomas, *Le Mort d'Arthur* (Hazleton, Pennsylvania: The Electronic Classics Series Publication, 2012)

Manni, Franco, 'A Eulogy of Finitude: Anthropology, Eschatology and Philosophy of History in Tolkien', in *The Broken Scythe: Death and Immortality in the Works of J.R.R. Tolkien*, ed. by Roberto Arduini and Claudio A. Testi (Zurich and Jena: Walking Tree Publishers, 2012), pp. 5–38

McDevitt, April, 'Color (iwen)', *Ancient Egypt: The Mythology* <http://www.egyptianmyths.net/colors.htm> [accessed 2 October 2016]

Reynolds, Pat, 'Death and Funerary Practices in Middle-earth', *The Tolkien Society* <https://www.tolkiensociety.org/wp-content/uploads/2016/11/Death-and-funerary-practices-in-Middle-earth.pdf> [accessed 5 October 2017]

Sandman, Lars, *A Good Death: On the Value of Death and Dying* (Maidenhead, Berkshire: Open University Press, 2005)

Shippey, T.A., *The Road to Middle-earth: How J.R.R. Tolkien Created a New Mythology* (London: Harper Collins, 1990)

The Romance of Tristan and Iseult, ed. by J. Bédier, trans. by H. Belloc (London: George Allen & Company, 1913)

'The Song of Roland', trans. by Jessie Crosland, *In Parentheses* (Cambridge, Ontario: In parentheses Publications, 1999) <http://www.yorku.ca/inpar/roland_crosland.pdf> [accessed 2 October 2016]

Weisman, A.D., and T.P. Hackett, 'Predilection to death. Death and dying as a psychiatric problem', *Psychosomatic Medicine*, 23 (1961), 232–56

The elven perspective of life, death and immortality, and its influence on humanity

Aslı Bülbül Candaş

Introduction

As an English man of letters who served in the British army in the First World War and was enlisted to become a code breaker in the Second, John Ronald Reuel Tolkien had been mingled with both world wars. In the First World War, during the Battle of the Somme, he parted from his wife and lost his good friends. He created his own universe and wrote the Middle-earth saga *The Lord of the Rings* before, during, and after the Second World War. He appreciated the value of life and understood the inevitableness of death to the highest degree that his thoughts and experiences of life and death were naturally reflected in his universe.

With respect to how immortality communes with the themes of life and death in Tolkien's literary works, this paper focuses on the Elves with each group of them at all ages of Arda. They have a completely different perception of space and time compared to Men, so their perspective of life and how it influences their actions in their lives are worth examining. At this point, the issue of the Half-elven makes the most important contribution to the triangle of life, death and immortality. The fact that they can choose their race means that they can choose their fate; whether to be mortal or immortal. For readers, they symbolize a much closer objective for humankind than common Elves do, and their right to choose presents the reader with the thought that human life gains meaning through death. In the history of Arda, there are three important couples who start or restore the Half-elven: Lúthien and Beren, Idril and Tuor, and Arwen and Aragorn. The wives are Elves whereas the husbands are Men. Lúthien and Arwen choose to be mortal whereas Idril is an exception as Tuor is presented with immortality.

The Half-elven

The first important Half-elven character in *The Silmarillion* is Dior Eluchíl whose parents are Beren and Lúthien. After the fall of , he raises the kingdom again although its existence is short, and the different characteristics of his ancestors help him to become a powerful figure in the history of Middle-earth. When he takes ownership of the Nauglamír, his appearance also proves his being Half-elven and the significance of this fact:

> Then Dior arose, and about his neck he clasped the Nauglamír; and now he appeared as the fairest of all the children of the world, of threefold race: of the Edain, and of the Eldar, and of the Maiar of the Blessed Realm. (*Silmarillion*, p. 236)

Then Eärendil Half-elven was born as the son of Idril and Tuor, and he turns out be a perfect representation of the advantages of being Half-elven: 'he had the beauty and the wisdom of the Eldar and the strength and hardihood of the Men of old' (*Silmarillion*, p. 241). It is no coincidence that Elwing, the daughter of Dior, and Eärendil, the son of Idril and Tuor, get married to each other, leading indirectly but successfully the last people of the Elves to the bitter end of the First Age and meanwhile manage to do a lot of important things, the most important of which is their sharing the situation of Middle-earth with the Valar and enabling the help of Aman to reach Middle-earth like passing the blessing of heaven to earth. As a common symbol of the Children of Ilúvatar, Eärendil takes an active part through the end of the War of Wrath against the dragons of Morgoth.

Eärendil's courage to step on to Aman is only possible thanks to his mixed race as can be understood from his explanation before his landing: 'Here none but myself shall set foot, lest you fall under the wrath of the Valar. But that peril I will take on myself alone, for the sake of the Two Kindreds' (*Silmarillion*, p. 248). Later, because of this step, Eärendil and Elwing are given the right to choose their race and so their fate openly by Manwë, and this is the first time for the Half-elven to decide on their matters of life, death and immortality. When the fact that both Eärendil and Elwing choose to be respected among the Elves is taken into consideration, it is obvious that their choice is led by their love for either their ancestors or each other.

The Half-elven who are in sight the most in *The Lord of the Rings* are Elrond and his children; his sons Elladan and Elrohir, and daughter Arwen. Their deeds in strategical timings show at what points the themes of life, death and immortality separate from each other and when they interlock. The lifestyles and choices of the Half-elven present the race of Men with an alternative race and culture and give them the motivation to spread on effort to transgress human-specific limitations at least.

The Edain and the Númenóreans

The Edain symbolize the other side of the coin as they are the Men closest to the Elves. They made a choice long ago and visited Beleriand, which was first inhabited by the Elves. Although their perception of time was no different than that of the other Men, they were introduced to a region which seemed special for the Elves, they were able to observe the lifestyles and philosophies of the Sindar and the exiled Noldor closely and they learned a lot from those Elves about the history of Arda, the Elvish tongues and the skills to produce unique artworks.

The different groups of Elves

The Elves who accept the summons to pass to the Undying Lands and those who stay in Middle-earth have different missions in their lives and different effects on the lives of Men as their perspective of immortality is slightly different. This seemingly small detail enables the Elves in Middle-earth to understand the inevitability of death for the race of Men clearly and closely. This fact is exhibited in detail at the time of Bëor's death:

> And when he lay dead, of no wound or grief, but stricken by age, the Eldar saw for the first time the swift waning of the life of Men, and the death of weariness which they knew not in themselves; and they grieved greatly for the loss of their friends. But Bëor at the last had relinquished his life willingly and passed in peace; and the Eldar wondered much at the strange fate of Men, for in all their lore there was no account

of it, and its end was hidden from them. (*Silmarillion*, p. 149)

Here the observation is basically made by the Noldor, the exiles who chose to return to Middle-earth after they had trouble in the Undying Lands.

According to the interpretation of Matthew Dickerson and Jonathan Evans, it is the Elves who choose to remain in Middle-earth who have the capacity to influence Men the most.[1] The Elves who remain faithful to this intention are my main area of interest in terms of inspiring Mankind. They are known as the Avari, also known as the Unwilling, the Sindar, the Nandor and the Noldor moving to Middle-earth at last.

The broadness of the elven perspective, its causes and effects

The Silmarillion

In order to understand the Elves' perspective of life, death and immortality, it is important to examine their culture from the very beginning of their race. First of all, in *The Silmarillion*, the collection of myths about Arda, in the first chapter 'Ainulindalë', they are named as 'the Firstborn' whereas Men are called 'the Followers'. It is obvious that Men should follow the Elves and should take their deeds as an example. The Elves are the first ones who are given the chance to observe Arda and appreciate the sea for the most part as they assume they can hear the Music of the Ainur in it. Their time on Arda starts long

---

[1] Matthew Dickerson and Jonathan Evans, *Ents, Elves, and Eriador* (Kentucky: The University Press of Kentucky, 2011).

before that of Men, they are presented as the leading race on it, and they are naturally immortal. From this perspective, they feel more closely related to the Valar than Men can do. The reader can see that clearly even in the details in *The Silmarillion*: 'Therefore the Valar may walk, if they will, unclad, and then even the Eldar cannot clearly perceive them, though they be present.' (*Silmarillion*, p. 21) If even the Eldar cannot sense the Valar, then Men are assumed to be weaker in their perception.

In addition, the Elves are the name givers to lots of things in Middle-earth for the first time. In *The Silmarillion*; frequently there are phrases like 'whom the Elves call' and 'which the Elves call'. Since Men come to Middle-earth after the Elves, they use the names that the Elves have found to call almost everything in their surroundings. This fact makes the Elves more familiar with Middle-earth and Men regard the Elves closer to the Valar. This familiarity does not prove Men to be in the wrong as from time to time, the Elves have the power to sense what will happen in the future of Middle-earth. One of the most important examples for this takes place just before the fall of Gondolin, the last kingdom of the Elves in the First Age. Turgon's daughter, Idril Celebrindal 'was wise and far-seeing, and her heart misgave her, and foreboding crept upon her spirit as a cloud.' (*Silmarillion*, p. 241) Therefore, the Elves could be considered as very competent on the matters of life, death and time.

The next important difference between the Elves and Men is about space perception. In *The Silmarillion*, the reader is introduced to the land of Aman where only the Elves are accepted by the Valar. The Elves are given the chance to live on this continent, so they have always known that they have a place to go other than Middle-earth and they can directly communicate with these immortal spirits. Moreover, as David Tneh remarks in his essay 'The Human Image and the Interrelationship of the Orcs, Elves and Men', if the Elves 'are killed, their spirits go to the Halls of Mandos.'[2] These privileges make them less greedy and more open minded than Men.

The other side of the coin

Nevertheless, things do not always go well for the Elves. As they have close relationships with the Valar and the Maiar, they feel both the benefits and harms of this situation. The Noldor, for instance, feel Melkor's doom the most while Men are merely influenced by the results of his actions. So, the Elves have good knowledge of both the mercy and the cruelty of the Maiar. As a matter of fact, the Elves have also made so many mistakes during their history and their present situation in *The Lord of the Rings* is a level they have reached by learning how to behave in accordance with their space and time perception which is much broader than that of Men. The Elves who have come from the West have the ability both to suppress their origin and to show it in Middle-earth, which is also a very interesting fact.

The Lord of the Rings

In *The Lord of the Rings*, there are three very important Elf characters. First of all, both Elrond and Galadriel have the ability to look at the Ring, its doom, and the probable solutions

---

[2] David Tneh, 'The Human Image and the Interrelationship of the Orcs, Elves and Men', *Mallorn*, 55 (2014), 35–39 (p. 38).

to get rid of it in perspective. They do not meet the possibility of death in the journey of the Ring with excitement but rather with deep knowledge, experience and tolerance unlike Men. It is important to understand the reason why the fellowship is constituted under the auspices of Elrond and why the council which makes the decision about the Ring is named 'The Council of Elrond'. Thanks to Elrond's knowledge and experience of the Ring, various creatures from different countries and regions of Middle-earth visit him to get advice. At this point, his long life enables him to make more practical and realistic decisions, and his perspective of life and death is so different than the other members of the council that he is the most successful character in focusing on the matter of the Ring. As for Arwen, she is the only Half-elven character who chooses to be mortal in *The Lord of the Rings*. Her choice of fate and future is a result of her love for Aragorn, and she is a symbol of real love who presents the reader with the reality that a long or eternal life is meaningless without this emotion, which she feels for a human.

The issue of free will

Upon the Elves' superiority over and influence on Men, there is one interesting point worth focusing on. According to the first draft version of 'Ainulindalë', it was not Tolkien's purpose to give the Elves the power of free will. Later on, it seems obvious that he changed his mind and gave them an indirect option of free will at least. The reason may be that on the one hand, he wanted the Elves to be like 'angels' of Christianity, holy beings who are meant to be obedient to God without questioning his decisions and wishes, and on the other hand, he designed the

Elves to be closer to Men than angels are to humans in the real world. Finally, the Elves have turned out to have indirect free will, and this fact has its roots just from the beginning of Eä with the music. As Troels Forchhammer mentions in his paper 'Voices of a Music: Models of Free Will in Tolkien's Middle-earth':

> not only do the actions of the Elves influence the choices of Men, but even the way they freely relate internally to their destined actions may influence the way that Men react to them. Through their interactions with Men, Elves are given a possibility to change the Music indirectly, and so the fate and the free will of Elves affect the free choices of Men which then have the power to affect the fate of both Elves and Men.[3]

So, the issue of free will is significant with regard to the relationship between the two races.

The Perfection of the Elves

The theological stand

As Tolkien has a certain Christian point of view, the lands which are open to the Elves in *The Silmarillion* can be in analogy of heaven, or afterlife in general, from the perspective of Men. The Elves always show the good side of afterlife as they are unchangeably good: 'there is no such thing as an evil

---

[3] Troels Forchhammer, 'Voices of a Music: Models of Free Will in Tolkien's Middle-earth', in *Freedom, Fate and Choice in Middle-earth*, ed. by Christopher Kreuzer, Peter Roe Series, XV (London: The Tolkien Society, 2008), pp. 10–25 (p. 20).

elf or a good orc in Tolkien'.[4] So the Elves mainly set a good example for Men with their broad provision of space and time compared to Men. Especially when the High Elves' blessed realm far from Middle-earth is called the Undying Lands, the word 'undying' is directly for the understanding of Men.

The physical characteristics of the Elves

The reflection of the Elves' perspective of life, death and immortality takes place most obviously in their physical appearance on Middle-earth. Since they regard time as almost a stabilized notion of the universe, their ageing is very slow accordingly. Their appearance which is a proof of their perspective has always been a popular theme in the scenes, but their perspective of life may be seldom underlined through Tolkien's books. What is more, this theme is one of the main elements of comparison between the Elves and Men. As Michael N. Stanton directly states in his book, *Hobbits, Elves, and Wizards*:

> High Elves, as Tolkien classifies such Elves as Elrond and Galadriel, are an idealized and elevated version of Men. [...] They seem perpetually youthful (Glorfindel: 'fair and young') or ageless (Elrond: 'neither young nor old'). Elrond's daughter Arwen is 'Young [...] and yet not so.'[5]

When the descriptions of Galadriel in the Middle-earth saga

---

[4] Richard Purtill, *Lord of the Elves and Eldils* (Michigan: Zondervan Corporation Grand Rapids, 1974), p. 102.
[5] Michael N. Stanton, *Hobbits, Elves, and Wizards* (New York: Palgrave Macmillan, 2002), p. 101.

are taken into consideration, it is not only their youth but also physical beauty which reflects the scope of their perspective. 'They resemble a "perfect" or almost perfect race of Men' and they are both mavens and symbols of beauty; such a combination seems to be mighty enough to examine in detail.[6]

Perfection in art

Art is another significant field with regard to the Elves' superiority over Men. Since the Elves are naturally immortal but for being killed, Tolkien did not let their deeds remain unfinished. If all the artworks of the Elves are examined in detail, it will become obvious that they are always completed perfectly. By trying to reach perfection in literature through the Elves, Tolkien inspires artists to reach perfection in art which is a thought leading the artist back to the Allegory of the Cave and *Defence of Poetry*.

If the race of Men is the one chained to the wall, the Elves are the ones outside who can observe the real nature. As philosophers, when they reach a certain level of understanding upon discovering the nature of reality, they turn back to the prisoners of the cave. From this standpoint, as the prisoners, Men should listen to the philosopher Elves without being afraid of facing with the reality. The things Men see in Middle-earth like its geographical features and the artworks of the Elves are nothing but the shadows, the reflections of the reality in Aman. Therefore, it is in Men's hands to quest for hitching their wagon to a star all the time.

By taking the artworks of the Elves as example, humans can

---

[6] Tneh, p. 38.

at least try to accept their mortality and realize their potential. As Roy W. Perrett specifies in his article:

> Most humans are deprived of the opportunity of realizing their potential. Thus for most the realization of this potential would require some form of continued personal life after death. In denying the reality of an afterlife, humanism is committed to the view that for the vast majority existence is in the end irredeemably tragic.[7]

Therefore, Tolkien also inspires all the people to express themselves through filling their lives with cultural productions.

Conclusion

What these facts, observations, deductions and impressions add to literature is the moment when the reader gradually realizes what inspires people of letters, artists, and mankind in general in Tolkien's legendarium. In his universe, the Elves set the pace for Men most of the time. Dickerson and Evans mention Tolkien's essay 'On Fairy-stories' and explain that 'what he says about our purpose relates closely to what we learned about the purpose of Elves in the mythology of Middle-earth.'[8]

The reader sees how the Elves' perspective of life, death and immortality is so different than that of Men, understands how Men would like to reach this level, and finally realizes that the Men of Middle-earth are no different than those of the real world. Therefore, this shift in the perspectives of the

---

[7] Roy W. Perrett, 'Regarding Immortality', *Religious Studies*, 22 (1986), 219–33 (p. 219).

[8] Dickerson and Evans, p. 36.

Elves and Men lead to a series of events throughout Tolkien's universe. The reader's journey in this universe reveals one of the most powerful ideals of humans, to be immortal and to see unreached places in our real universe.

Works Consulted

Anderson, Poul, 'Awakening the Elves', in *Meditations on Middle-earth*, ed. by Karen Haber (London: Simon & Schuster, 2003), pp. 21–31

Dickerson, Matthew, and Jonathan Evans, *Ents, Elves, and Eriador* (Kentucky: The University Press of Kentucky, 2011)

Forchhammer, Troels, 'Voices of a Music: Models of Free Will in Tolkien's Middle-earth', in *Freedom, Fate and Choice in Middle-earth*, ed. by Christopher Kreuzer, Peter Roe Series, xv (London: The Tolkien Society, 2008), pp. 10–25

Perrett, Roy W., 'Regarding Immortality', *Religious Studies*, 22 (1986), 219–33

Purtill, Richard, *Lord of the Elves and Eldils* (Michigan: Zondervan Corporation Grand Rapids, 1974)

Stanton, Michael N., *Hobbits, Elves, and Wizards* (New York: Palgrave Macmillan, 2002)

Tneh, David, 'The Human Image and the Interrelationship of the Orcs, Elves and Men', *Mallorn*, 55 (2014), 35–39

Mortal immortals: the fallibility of elven immortality in Tolkien's writing

Anna Milon

Tolkien describes his writing, especially *The Lord of the Rings*, as being primarily 'concerned with Death, and Immortality; and the "escapes": serial longevity, and hoarding memory' (*Letters*, p. 235). Since immortality is an 'exemption from death' according to the *Oxford English Dictionary*,[1] one would think it is opposite to death, but Tolkien places immortality and death side by side, identifying 'serial longevity, and hoarding memory' as the escapes from both. Verlyn Flieger explains that the two terms are evidence of the author 'working around any mention of reincarnation',[2] as reincarnation would be seen as unorthodox according to the Catholic doctrine. 'Hoarding memory', according to Flieger, is a 'psychic or psychological connector/channel between characters in the narrative present and the distant past beyond their waking memory'.[3] For example, in two of Tolkien's abandoned endeavours 'The Lost Road' and 'The Notion Club Papers', 'two modern-day Englishmen travel back to Númenor through the unconscious memories of a succession of ever more ancient forebears'.[4] 'Serial longevity' is referred to as 'rebirth' (*Morgoth*, p. 218) in

---

[1] 'immortality, n.', *Oxford English Dictionary* <www.oed.com> [accessed 12 March 2016].

[2] Verlyn Flieger, 'The Curious Incident of the Dream at the Barrow: Memory and Reincarnation in Middle-earth', in her *Green Suns and Faerie* (Kent, OH: The Kent State University Press, 2012), pp. 89–101 (p. 93).

[3] *Ibid.*, p. 90.

[4] *Ibid.*

Tolkien's later writing. Flieger attributes this change of terms to Tolkien leaving 'the concept safely confined to imaginary beings', since the process of rebirth (and therefore, immortality) is only available to Elves.[5] However, despite this and various other abilities available to the Elves, their escape from death is ultimately an unsuccessful one.

'The "Elves" are "immortal", at least as far as this world goes' (*Silmarillion*, p. xiv). What is 'this' world that the writer refers to: Middle-earth, the whole of Arda encompassing both Middle-earth and the Undying Lands, or the world in which Tolkien is writing a letter to his friend Milton Waldman? Tolkien continues that these 'immortal' Elves 'are concerned rather with the griefs and burdens of deathlessness in time and change, than with death' (*Silmarillion*, p. xiv); while they are unconcerned with death, they are not exempt from it, as 'there were times of great trouble [...]; and Death afflicted all the Eldar, as it did all other living things in Arda' (*Morgoth*, p. 218). Therefore, Elves are not immortal in the conventional sense.

Tolkien, who at first presents a straightforward claim that 'no living person incarnate may be without a *fëa*,[6] nor without a *hrondo*,[7] deliberately problematizes the dichotomy between living characters and dead ones. The use of the word 'incarnate'

---

[5] *Ibid.*

[6] The soul, it 'cannot be broken or disintegrated by any violence from without' (*Morgoth*, p. 218). Elsewhere, Tolkien theorises that the *fea* is 'not destructible within its appointed term, but when that [is] reached it cease[s] to be' (*Morgoth*, p. 332). He appends that this is a theory that only 'Some argued' (*Morgoth*, p. 332).

[7] The physical body, it 'can be hurt and may be utterly destroyed' (*Morgoth*, p. 218).

suggests that there are characters who are living, but without a body. However, no characters within Tolkien's writing are explicitly referred to as both alive and disembodied. Instead, Tolkien describes various modes of consciousness: existing after the separation of the *fëa* from the *hrondo*. For example, Miriel, whose body 'remained unwithered' (*Silmarillion*, p. 64) after the soul left it, exists in a vegetative state of a living body without a consciousness; the Army of the Dead, who have been cursed 'to rest never until [their] oath is fulfilled' (*RK*, V, ii), have 'slowly dwindled in the barren hills' (*RK*, V, ii) physically, but continue to walk Middle-earth as spirits; the Nazgul have fallen under the influence of the Great Rings, but although they did not die a physical death, they have become 'invisible permanently and [walk] in the twilight under the eye of the dark power that rules the Rings' (*FR*, I, ii). Tolkien does not equate being alive with being conscious. The 'destruction of the *hrondo* [causes] death or the unhousing of the *fëa*' (*Morgoth*, p. 218), but the fëa remains conscious and is 'open to the direct instruction and command of the Valar' (*Morgoth*, p. 219). Characters like the Ring-wraiths, who are comprised of 'will' and have no physical bodies, cannot be considered truly alive.[8] In Tolkien's universe characters have access to more states of existence than 'being alive' and therefore having agency and awareness, or 'being dead' and therefore having no consciousness and no agency.

All these characters exist in the liminal space between the living and the dead, and partially erase the boundary between the two. Because of them, death stops being the feared Great

---

[8] Éowyn calls the Witch-king of Angmar a 'dwimmerlaik' (*RK*, V, vi) which Tolkien glosses as 'work of necromancy, spectre' (*RK*, Index).

Unknown. Characters can envisage what may happen to them after they die and even hope to meet their deceased loved ones, whose *fëa* and *hrondo* have already been rent asunder. Tolkien writes on several occasions that fear of death itself is unnatural, that death 'is but the name we give to that which Melkor had tainted, and it sounds therefore evil, but untainted its name would be good' (*Morgoth*, p. 314). As Gandalf says in Peter Jackson's cinematic adaptation, 'death is just another path, one that we all must take'.[9] But once the fear of death is allayed, it is replaced by another fear. The fear of decrepitude and barrenness. Such is the fear of Denethor, who claims that he is 'old but not yet dotard' (*RK*, V, iv); and of Aragorn, whose wisdom demands he goes with good grace before he falls from his high seat 'unmanned and witless' (*RK*, Appendix A, I, v). The anxiety of outliving one's capacity is summed up eloquently in Éowyn's fear of 'a cage [...] to stay behind bars, until use and old age accept them, and all chance of doing great deeds is gone beyond recall or desire' (*RK*, V, ii). For the Elves outliving their time is one of the conditions of their existence.

Their native land, Valinor is a land of immortality, where 'naught faded nor withered' (*Silmarillion*, p. 38). However, Tolkien names, consciously or unconsciously, the West 'Annun', after the Celtic Underworld, creating the association between Valinor and death. Aman and the Sundering Seas that separate it from Middle-earth are established as 'a word of fear' and 'a token of death' (*FR*, Prologue) among the Hobbits. Upon closer inspection, it becomes apparent that the lack of decay in Valinor is also the lack of change. Tolkien writes that, '"change"

---

[9] *The Lord of the Rings: The Return of the King*, dir. by Peter Jackson (New Line Cinema, 2003).

[is] viewed as a regrettable thing' (*Silmarillion*, p. xxii) by the Elves and that their chief motive is the 'preservation of what is desired or loved, or its semblance' (Silmarillion, p. xxii). Unlike the turbulent Middle-earth, Valinor remains unchanged throughout the ages of Arda. Anything that is destroyed in it is replaced by a lesser semblance of itself: the light-giving trees Telperion and Laurelin are succeeded by the Moon (a single flower of Telperion) and the Sun (Laurelin's fruit). No greater things are created in Valinor after its Noontide in the First Age. Despite this seeming immortality, the Elven existence is one of slow and irreversible decay. Their affinity with Arda and the ability to have 'the greater bliss in the world' comes at the cost of the finiteness of their experience. By the Third Age, the Elves outlive their capacity in Middle-earth and must depart it. Tolkien writes that 'if the Elves would not come to the western shores and tarried in the lands of men, then they should slowly fade and fail' (*Morgoth*, p. 218).

Fading is another phenomenon significant of Elven mortality. You may be most familiar with it in the case of Arwen. After the death of Aragorn, she departs to Lothlórien and lays herself up on Cerin Amroth, 'and there is her green grave until the world is changed' (*RK*, Appendix A, I, v). Fading appears to be a process of voluntary death following a great trauma or exertion of the spirit, such as in the case of Arwen or Miriel. However, Tolkien also writes in the 'Laws and Customs of the Eldar', that 'as ages passed the dominance of [the Elves'] *fëar* ever increased, "consuming" their bodies […]. The end of this process is their "fading" […]; for the body becomes at last, as it were, a memory held by the *fëa* […] so the Elves are indeed deathless and may not be destroyed or changed' (*Morgoth*, p. 219) It is unclear what happens to the body after fading: it may either become invisible, but remain tangible, like the Nazgûl, or it may be arrested in its optimal state and no longer undergo physical change. A clue is given in the discourse of Finrod and Andreth: 'the living eyes may draw from the *fëa* within an image which the houseless conveys to the housed: the memory of itself' (*Morgoth*, p. 353). This suggests that when a living being sees a faded soul, it may appear as a spectre of the body it had when alive. In any case, according to Tolkien's logic of the union of *fëa* and *hrondo* equalling life, faded Elves are immortal. Because their bodies become extensions of their souls and can no longer be separated. However, Tolkien does not countermand the idea of fading as death. Perhaps the faded Elves are only deathless because they have died already. Yet, having died, they continue to exist, to be conscious.

In that, Elves appear to be the opposites of mortals. Their bodies are able to survive indefinitely, but their souls are finite as opposed to the mortal frail bodies and infinite souls. In the dialogue of Finrod and Andreth, the work considered by Christopher Tolkien to be his father's definitive word on mortality, Tolkien writes that

Elvish 'immortality' is bounded within a part of Time (which [one] would call the History of Arda), and is therefore strictly to be called rather 'serial longevity', the utmost limit of which is the length of the existence of Arda. [...] A corollary of this is that the Elvish *fëa* is also limited to the Time of Arda, or at least held within it and unable to leave it, while it lasts. (*Morgoth*, p. 331)

Tolkien follows it with a statement that 'All the Elves would then "die" at the End of Arda' (*Morgoth*, p. 331), because their purpose in Ilúvatar's plan will be fulfilled. Thus, whatever path the Elves choose—to stay in Middle-earth to a slow failing of the spirit or to abide in Valinor for a prolonged while but not forever before they are dissolved—both their souls and their bodies are finite unlike any others in Tolkien's universe.

So far, only the personal immortality of the Elves, the survival of each individual identity, has been scrutinized. But philosopher Eugene Fontinell names at least five other types of immortality:

> absolute spirit immortality (we are immortal insofar as we are absorbed within the Eternal Spirit, or Everlasting God, or the One, etc.); cosmic immortality (we are immortal insofar as we emerge from and return to the cosmos or nature); ideal immortality (we are immortal insofar as we participate in timeless values or eternal ideals); achievement immortality (we are immortal through our creative acts or deeds); posterity immortality (we are immortal through our children, or the community or the race).[10]

Tolkien goes to some lengths to ensure that his Elves are not immortal according to any of the categories mentioned above. Individually, they are afflicted by the death of the body. Cosmically, their role in Eru's plan is finite; and so is the cosmos of Arda which they inhabit. Their offspring vanish from Middle-earth. And with the last ship sailing to the West, 'an end comes to the Eldar of story and song' (*Silmarillion*, p. 383), confining their creative acts and ideals to oblivion. It is possible that Tolkien avoids the term 'reincarnation' not just because it is unorthodox, but because he opposes the idea of perpetuity altogether. The Elves may live indefinitely, but, like

---

[10] Eugine Fontinell, 'Immortality: Hope or Hindrance?', *CrossCurrents*, 31 (1981), 163–84 (p. 165).

the bearers of the Great Rings, they do not gain more life, nor change with the time. The Elven 'fading', universal to the race in the Third Age, is a state of living death, a perpetuity spent in stasis.

What then of the 'immortal mortals', the characters who live a short while and die of old age, but who are in possession of an immortal soul? Tolkien's Men believe that they are 'born to life everlasting, without any shadow of any end' (*Morgoth*, p. 314). Rather than 'everlasting life', it is 'everlasting being' that Tolkien's mortals are born into. Their souls, although divorced from physical bodies, 'cannot be broken or disintegrated' (*Morgoth*, p. 218) until the end of Arda. And after the end, those souls will be accepted into the choir of the Second Song, coming into contact with God—Eru, who will 'give to their thoughts the secret fire' (*Silmarillion*, p. 4)—a creative power of their own.

Works Consulted

Oxford English Dictionary, <www.oed.com> [accessed 12 March 2016]

Flieger, Verlyn, 'Over a Bridge of Time', in her *A Question of Time: J.R.R. Tolkien's Road to Faerie* (Kent, OH: The Kent State University Press, 1997), pp. 89–116

——, 'The Curious Incident of the Dream at the Barrow: Memory and Reincarnation in Middle-earth', in her *Green Suns and Faerie* (Kent, OH: The Kent State University Press, 2012), pp. 89–101

Fontinell, Eugine, 'Immortality: Hope or Hindrance?', *CrossCurrents*, 31 (1981), 163–84

Gifts in harmony? A philological exploration of Tolkien's invented words for 'life' and 'death'

Andrew Higgins

In his legendarium Tolkien tells how the two children of Ilúvatar, the firstborn Elves and the second born Men came to be in Arda as well as they are each fated to eventually leave it. In this short paper, using Tolkien's foundational statement from the drafts of his *On Fairy-stories* 'mythology is language and language is mythology' (*OFS*, p. 181), I want to explore how Tolkien used his coeval language invention to construct base roots and associated words which would enter the legendarium primarily through names for people and places to both signify and commemorate these two key events.

When it comes to describing the birth of Elves and Men, Tolkien constructs two key place names that have within them some of the key mythic concepts that Tolkien describes in the narratives of these origin stories which first appear in *The Book of Lost Tales*. The key mythic theme that both these origin stories emphasize is that both Elves and the Fathers of Men were not created in Arda but awoke; their creation being achieved off stage as it were by Ilúvatar himself. This mythic theme is apparent in two key place names where this awakening occurs: Koivie-neni (later to become known as Cuiviénen) and Murmenalda.

At the heart of the first place name is the early Qenya base root KOYO from which Tolkien constructs words which connect the ideas of live, living and coming to life with awakening.[1] The early form of this place name itself is formed from a gerundial form of one of these words and another base root for water; NENE possibly meaning flow.[2] Starting in Gnomish and then into the Noldorin language of the 1920s (the precursor to Sindarin) the /ko/ phoneme becomes /cu/ from which Tolkien constructs a series of related words including a Gnomish name for this place of awakening 'Nenin a Gwivros' (*Lost Tales I*, p. 257); still meaning 'waters of awakening'. In 'The Etymologies' of 1938 the Qenya base root KOYO becomes the Eldarin proto-root KUY (*Lost Road*, p. 366) with the association of the ideas of coming to life by awakening persisting; as in the later Quenya form of this place name — Cuiviénen now parsed by Tolkien as cuivië 'awakening' + nen 'water'.

This sense of 'awakening' begs the question what did the Elves awaken from? In the earliest conceptual versions of this tale there is evidence that there was more to this awakening. In *The Book of Lost Tales*, Manwë asks the embassy of Elves 'Tell us how ye came; how found ye the world' (*Lost Tales I*, p. 116) one of the Elves Nolemë responds 'For meseems I awoke but now from a long sleep eternally profound whose vast dreams are already forgotten' (*Lost Tales I*, p. 116). Another Elf, Tinwë says 'thereto his heart told him that he was new-come from illimitable regions, yet he might not recollect by what dark and strange paths he had been brought' (*Lost Tales I*, p. 116). In his commentary to this passage, Christopher Tolkien states

---

[1] J.R.R. Tolkien, 'Qenyaqetsa: The Qenya Phonology and Lexicon: together with The Poetic and Mythologic Words of Eldarissa', ed. by Christopher Gilson, Carl Hostetter, Patrick Wynne and Arden R. Smith, *Parma Eldalamberon*, 12 (1998), 1–121 (p. 48).

[2] *Ibid.*, p. 65.

'The story of the questioning of the three Elves by Manwë concerning the nature of their coming into the world, and their loss of all memory of what preceded by their awakening, did not survive the Lost Tales' (*Lost Tales I*, p. 132). And indeed, in later conceptual versions of this story the Elves just awake with no real sense or exploration of what they have awakened from. However, there is an intriguing fragment that the late Tolkien scholar Taum Santoski discovered in the Tolkien archives at Marquette University on the back of some papers that Tolkien was drafting for 'The Riders of Rohan' chapter of *The Lord of the Rings* (c. early 1940s) which was published by the Elvish Linguistic Fellowship in *Vinyar Tengwar*; which states in Quenya 'Eldar ando kakainen loralyar Koivienenissen' (the Elves were long lying asleep at Koivieneni).[3] The word for 'asleep' in this fragment 'loralyar' is derived from the base root LORO which in *The Qenya Lexicon* and later 'Etymologies' is one of the variant forms used to construct words having to do both with sleeping (as in the Qenya verb lor- meaning to slumber) as well as dreaming (as in the related olor [dream], the realm of Lórien the king of dreams and the Istar Olórin [Gandalf]).[4] The place names Koivieneni and later Cuiviénen formed from that key base root marks and signifies this act of awakening with an echo of forgotten dreams which only seemingly remains, and more importantly can only be revealed, by understanding the way Tolkien signifies it through his language invention.

The genesis of men in Tolkien's mythology, as with their

---

[3] J.R.R. Tolkien, 'The Elves at Koivienéni: A New Quenya Sentence', ed. by Christopher Gilson and Patrick Wynne, *Vinyar Tengwar*, 14 (1990), 5–7, 12–20.

[4] Tolkien, 'Qenyaqetsa', p. 63; *Lost Road*, p. 370.

ultimate fate, is far murkier. Probably the most extensive treatment in the mythology is again in *The Book of Lost Tales*. Here it is one of the Elves (Nuin) who stays behind from the Great March who comes upon a place in the East called Murmenalda 'the Vale of Sleep' (*Lost Tales I*, pp. 232–33) which contains sleeping forms 'and some were twined each in the other's arms and some lay sleeping gently all alone, and Nuin stood and marveled scarce breathing' (*Lost Tales I*, pp. 232–33). As with the morphological construction of the place name Cuiviénen, the place name Murmenalda also signifies this act of sleeping, dreaming and awakening from sleep. At the morphological heart of this place name is the base root MURU which in The Qenya Lexicon means just 'to slumber'.[5] In The Gnomish Lexicon, Tolkien uses the same form to construct the verb 'murtha' to dream and the related word 'mure' meaning a nightmare or vision of the night.[6] Thus through language invention Tolkien links the ideas of slumbering and dreaming. A form of mur is used to form the name of the abode of the Valar of dreams Luriel or Lórien as well. Thus the place name Murmenalda is grounded in ideas around both sleeping and dreaming and Tolkien reinforces this in the text by having Murmenalda 'full of sweet fragrances and songs of nightingales' (*Lost Tales I*, p. 233); a close parallel to his description of the abode of Lórien the Vala of dreams in Valinor. In later conceptual versions of the legendarium, the birth of Men is not widely described and by the time of 'The Etymologies' the word 'maur' has come to signify gloom (*Lost*

---

[5] Tolkien, 'Qenyaqetsa', p. 63.

[6] J.R.R. Tolkien, 'I-Lam-na-Ngoldathon: The Grammar and Lexicon of the Gnomish Tongue', ed. by Christopher Gilson, Patrick Wynne, Arden R. Smith and Carl Hostetter, *Parma Eldalamberon*, 11 (1995), p. 58.

Road, p. 373).

However, if Elves and Men share a common type of origin in their coming into Arda, their leaving it is a key differentiating fate that is at the core of Tolkien's mythos. As Tolkien said in a letter about his legendarium, 'The real theme for me is about something much more permanent and difficult: Death and Immortality: the mystery of the love of the world in the hearts of a race "doomed" to leave and seemingly love it; the anguish in the hearts of a race "doomed" not to leave it; until its whole evil-aroused story is complete' (*Letters*, p. 246). Starting in In *The Book of Lost Tales*, Tolkien wrote that 'The Eldar dwell [in the world] till the Great End unless they be slain or waste in grief (for to both of these deaths are they subject), nor doth eld subdue their strength, except it may be in ten thousands centuries; and dying they are reborn in their children, so that their numbers minish not, nor grow' (*Lost Tales I*, p. 59). Elvish fate was to remain in Arda until the end of their world (what Tolkien calls 'the Great End') and a key concept attached to this duration is the fading of the Elves. Men on the other hand die and are given then gift and freedom to go beyond the circles of the world. On his death-bed Aragorn says to his beloved Arwen 'Behold! We are not bound for ever to the circles of world, and beyond them is more than memory' (*RK*, Appendix A, I, v).

To linguistically describe and distinguish the fates of Elves and Men, Tolkien invented several base roots to construct words that would signify these contrasting aspects. In some cases, these roots and attendant words can apply to methods of death Elves and Men share; namely being killed or slain in battle. While in others Tolkien invents base roots and attendant words that delineate the differences in Elvish and mortal death. As I will show these more specific aspects of these deaths become more focused and honed when some of these key Qenya base roots were adapted by Tolkien into 'The Etymologies' of the late 1930s; that great linguistic expression of Tolkien's growing tree of Elvish tongues from which he would construct many of the Elvish words found in *The Lord of the Rings*.

The slaying of the Elves and Men in Arda (primarily in battle) is signified by the early Qenya base root MAKA from which Tolkien constructs the verb for slaughter 'makta-' and noun 'makka' as well as the name for the early Vala of battle Makar and several words for sword which is also reflected in several of the related Gnomish words Tolkien invented.[7] In 'The Etymologies' this Qenya base root becomes the proto-Eldarin root MAK; now having a slightly more focused meaning of specifically 'sword or as verb-stem to fight with a sword' (*Lost Road*, p. 371). Whereas a new Proto-Eldarin base root in the 'Etymologies' signifies being slain NDAK (*Lost Road*, p. 375) from which Tolkien constructs related Elvish words such as the Old Noldorin verb ndakie 'to slay' and *ndango* 'slain' which in Noldorin became such related words as degi 'to slay' and doen 'corpse'.

The significance of the key fate of the Elves to remain in Arda until the Great End and in sense to die by fading, grief or weariness (what Christopher Tolkien in his commentary called a type of Elvish death) is signified by two key base roots that Tolkien first invented in The Qenya Lexicon and then continued to develop in the different conceptual phases of his language invention as he focused the ideas around Elvish 'death' that they were each expressing. They first appear as the Qenya base

---

[7] Tolkien, 'Qenyaqetsa', pp. 57–58.

roots QALA and QELE.[8]

QALA starts out just meaning 'die' and from which Tolkien constructs words for death, dead and deadly. QELE also means die but also 'perish, decay and fail' and some of the words that Tolkien constructs from this base root are words for perish, ruin, utter end and corpse and carcass. In 'The Etymologies' Tolkien brings the QALA Qenya base root in now as proto-Eldarin root KWAL (*Lost Road*, p. 366) where he gives it a more specific meaning of 'die in pain' and suggests the same Qenya word 'qalme' to mean death but now adds the idea of agony to it. But in an interesting note in this entry of 'The Etymologies' Tolkien states that in Noldorin another base root replaced KWAL in developing words around agony and death. This base root is WAN meaning 'depart, go away, disappear, and vanish' (*Lost Road*, p. 397) which also becomes associated with words around death and being departed. WAN itself is an interesting proto-root in itself as it both suggests the English word 'wan' which means pale, gloomy, and faded coming from the Old English word wann 'dark, black' and also in Tolkien's own Elvish looks back to a related earlier Qenya base root VAHA from which Tolkien constructed several words for going away, things being past, over, and lost from which the word *vanwa* comes which finds its way into the name of the house of the Elves on Tol Eressëa—Mar Vanwa Tyliéva (The Cottage of Lost Play).[9] Thus in the application of this base root in Noldorin (the language of the exiled Elves), Tolkien brings together through these two proto-roots the ideas of agony, pain in death with the fading and weariness of the Elves (suggesting

---

[8] *Ibid.*, p. 76.
[9] *Ibid.*, p. 99.

115

the above idea of wasting in grief). This linking of feeling pain and agony with fading appears in the late dialogue about Elvish and mortal death — 'Athrabeth Finrod ah Andreth' — when the mortal Andreth says to the Elf Finrod 'what know ye of death? To you it may be in pain, it may be bitter and a loss—but only for a time' (*Morgoth*, p. 317).

The other base root QELE which means 'perish, die, decay and fail' follows a similar linguistic trajectory that focuses it more on the idea of fading. The first focusing of this root can be seen The Gnomish Lexicon where Tolkien posits there is a reconstructed word (an asterisk word) cwel which now specifically means 'fade, wither'.[10] In 'The Etymologies' QELE becomes the proto-Eldarin base root KWEL (*Lost Road*, p. 366) and Tolkien specifically associates it with the title of his earliest poem composed in Qenya in March 1916 'Narqelion' (now being given a new specific meaning as 'fire-fading') which is glossed as 'autumn' and is a poem about fading and withering of both the seasons, trees and the Elves. In some notes for this entry in 'The Etymologies', published in *Vinyar Tengwar* 45, Tolkien also constructs the word 'lassekwelene' meaning 'leaf-fading' suggesting it as an alternative to 'Lasse-lanta' and 'Narqelion'—fire fading.[11] So the base root QELE/KWEL like QALA/KWAL seems to have become more specifically associated with the fading of the Elves and the agony and grief that this caused as part of their fate to remain with the circles of Arda until the Great End. The fact that Tolkien invented two Qenya base roots which persisted in varying forms shows that

---

[10] Tolkien, 'I-Lam-na-Ngoldathon', p. 28.

[11] J.R.R. Tolkien, 'Addenda and Corrigenda to the Etymologies—Part One', ed. by Carl Hostetter and Patrick Wynne, *Vinyar Tengwar*, 45 (2003), 3–38 (p. 24).

this was a key concept for the Elves to have many different and nuanced words to describe in their languages.

Thus since these two early roots throughout the process of Tolkien's Elvish language conception become more focused on the specific Elvish fate of fading, in his development of 'The Etymologies' Tolkien invented another specific proto-Eldarin root to signify in Elvish the death of Men; namely PHIR (*Lost Road*, p. 381) from which comes the Elvish words for being dead by natural causes (Q. Firin), mortals (firima), human (firya). Most intriguingly the word for 'natural death (as an act)' is 'faire' and the noun for 'dead' is 'fern'. In a related note in 'The Etymologies' Tolkien wrote in the margin 'PHIR die of natural causes—not as Elves hence Q. Firma mortal' (*Lost Road*, p. 381). In terms of the word 'faire' meaning 'death by natural act' there may be an interesting link here to an older Qenya base root FAYA which in The Qenya Lexicon forms the words 'faire' meaning 'free and freedom'.[12] This suggests that Tolkien may be linking the two key ideas of mortal death and freedom from the circles of the world. In the original 'Music of the Ainur' death for men is called 'the freedom to go beyond the original Music' (*Lost Tales I*, p. 59). Another word in this entry is 'fern' the noun for dead. As an interesting (although tentative connection) this same word form appears in Sir John Rhys's 1884 work *Celtic Britain* in which Rhys reported that the language of the pre-Celtic aboriginal inhabitants of the British Isles (which Rhys calls 'Ivernian') was preserved in a glossary by an Irish 'king-bishop' of Casel Cormac mac Cuilennain (died 908). He did record two words known to

---

[12] Tolkien, 'Qenyaqetsa', p. 37.

him: fern, anything good and ond, a stone.[13] As several Tolkien scholars have explored, Tolkien remembered reading this passage by Sir John Rhys when he was inventing his lexicon and clearly the 'ond' stone was one Tolkien would use in his name invention (e.g. Gondolin, Gondor, etc). Since doing my PhD thesis I have been searching throughout the corpus for where Tolkien may have used 'fern anything good' and this is the closest I have come to it. Is there a suggestion here that death for men (i.e. being able to leave the circles of the world and go beyond) was originally a good thing that was perverted by the evil of Melkor? Indeed, as the mortal Andreth says in the 'Athrabeth' 'death is but the name that we give to something that he [Melkor] has tainted, and it sounds therefore evil, but untainted its name would be good' (*Morgoth*, p. 314). Death for man was originally a good thing, indeed it was (and possibly is) a gift to leave the circles of the world. Men were just guests (as the Elves called them) in Arda and had an ultimate unknown to all, which was a good thing until it was perverted by Melkor. This proto-Eldarin root also becomes associated with the place name Dor finn I guinar 'the Land of the Dead that Live' which in the Beren and Lúthien cycle of stories is where they both lived after their return from the dead and Lúthien's choice to live as a mortal woman for the rest of the days. A name that Lúthien becomes known by in her later days is Firiel, which is Quenya for 'mortal-woman', is formed from this key base root as well.

Tolkien's invention of several key base roots and related words to signify the different aspects of both Elvish and mortal

[13] John Rhys, *Celtic Britain* (London: Society for Promotion of Christian Knowledge, 1884), p. 270.

death shows how complex and interwoven this theme was in the mythic structure of Tolkien's legendarium. As with the roots and words for how Elves and Men entered Arda, while the words for death makes certain distinctions they also show some shared themes of the two gifts that Ilúvatar gave to Elves and Men. In both cases Elves and Men will die—as stated in the 'Athrabeth': 'Men had a shadow behind them, but the Elves had a shadow before them' (*Morgoth*, p. 314). Men die and leave the circles of the world but Elves too will die at the end of Arda—what happens next for both races only is known to Ilúvatar himself.

Through his imaginative process of combined, coeval and intertwined mytho- and glosso- poeia Tolkien depicted how the two children of Ilúvatar came to be in and leave Arda—two gifts in harmony given to Elves and the fathers of Men who both awoke in Arda and would eventually though the paths of their own fates come back together beyond the end of time.

Works Consulted

Rhys, John, *Celtic Britain* (London: Society for Promotion of Christian Knowledge, 1884)

Tolkien, J.R.R., 'The Elves at Koivienéni: A New Quenya Sentence', ed. by Christopher Gilson and Patrick Wynne, *Vinyar Tengwar*, 14 (1990), 5–7, 12–20

——, 'I-Lam-na-Ngoldathon: The Grammar and Lexicon of the Gnomish Tongue', ed. by Christopher Gilson, Patrick Wynne, Arden R. Smith and Carl Hostetter, *Parma Eldalamberon*, 11 (1995)

——, 'Qenyaqetsa: The Qenya Phonology and Lexicon: together with The Poetic and Mythologic Words of Eldarissa', ed. by Christopher Gilson, Carl Hostetter, Patrick Wynne and Arden R. Smith, *Parma Eldalamberon*, 12 (1998), 1–121

——, 'Addenda and Corrigenda to the Etymologies—Part One', ed. by Carl Hostetter and Patrick Wynne, *Vinyar Tengwar*, 45 (2003), 3–38

Music of life: the creation of Middle-earth

Sarah Rose

> Then the voices of the Ainur, like unto harps and lutes, and pipes and trumpets, and viols and organs, and like unto countless choirs singing with words, began to fashion the theme of Ilúvatar to a great music; and a sound arose of endless interchanging melodies woven in harmony that passed beyond hearing into the depths and into the heights, and the places of the dwelling of Ilúvatar were filled to overflowing, and the music and the echo of the music went out into the Void, and it was not void. (*Silmarillion*, p. 15)

These words are from the beginning of *The Silmarillion*. Like all great mythologies, *The Silmarillion* begins with the story of creation. Before the Great Music, before the Ainur, there is Eru, the One, who is called Ilúvatar. He creates the Ainur, the Holy Ones, and proposes to them themes of music. The Ainur sing their primordial song, then Ilúvatar says, '"Behold your music!" And he showed to them a vision, giving to them sight where before was only hearing' (*Silmarillion*, p. 17). The Ainur saw Arda in this vision and saw how their own part in the Great Music had helped to shape the world. Then Ilúvatar turned the vision into reality, saying, 'Eä! Let these things Be!' (*Silmarillion*, p. 20). Thus Ilúvatar brought music out of silence, light out of darkness, and a world out of nothing. Many of the Ainur descended to the world and are called the Valar or Powers, and they helped to fashion and give order to the world. Thus Arda and within it Middle-earth came to be.

The creation story presented in *The Silmarillion* is truly

unique. It is a new mythology. But like all great myths, it presents answers to some of life's biggest questions. How did the world come to be? Who created the world? Is the creator good, and if so, why is there evil in the world? Or did no one create the world, and life came about through the big bang, evolution, or some other random event in a random universe? These questions are not just for scientists and theologians, nor even just for poets and professors like Tolkien. Mankind always and everywhere has asked these questions, for if we do not know where we came from, how can we know where we are going?

Most myths present some answer to these questions. Although Tolkien's mythology is highly creative and not drawn from any one source, it nonetheless contains a few echoes from other creation stories. This paper will examine four such stories: first, Völuspá, the Norse myth found in the Poetic Edda; second, the creation account at the beginning of the Finnish epic the Kalevala; third, the 'Harmony of the Spheres', a concept first proposed by the Greek philosopher and mathematician Pythagoras, taken up by St Augustine and Boethius; and fourth, the creation account in scripture found in the book of Genesis. After these sources are examined, Tolkien's own myth might be seen in a new light, or heard in a different key.

Völuspá is the first poem of the Poetic Edda, a collection of Norse mythology written around the tenth century and passed down orally for many years before that. In Völuspá, alternatively Voluspo or 'The Wise-Woman's Prophecy', a female seer speaks to Odin, who has sought her out to learn more about Ragnarök, the great battle of gods and giants that is forthcoming. The seer predicts many events of Ragnarök, but first she speaks of the creation of the world.

> Of old was the age ǁ when Ymir lived;
> Sea nor cool waves ǁ nor sand there were;
> Earth had not been, ǁ nor heaven above,
> But a yawning gap, ǁ and grass nowhere.[1]

Ymir was a giant. When he lived, before the world was fashioned, there was no sea, nor earth, nor heaven, but a yawning gap or void. Out of the body of Ymir the giant, the gods carved the world.

> Then Bur's sons lifted ǁ the level land,
> Mithgarth the mighty ǁ there they made;
> The sun from the south ǁ warmed the stones of earth,
> And green was the ground ǁ with growing leeks.
> [...]
> Then sought the gods ǁ their assembly-seats,
> The holy ones, ǁ and council held;
> Names then gave they ǁ to noon and twilight,
> Morning they named, ǁ and the waning moon,
> Night and evening, ǁ the years to number.[2]

Bur's sons were Othin or Odin, Vili, and Ve; together they formed Mithgarth, or Middle-earth, the world of men. After the world is fashioned, the gods hold council and give names to morning, noon, and night. The gods are at peace for a time until the arrival of three giant-maidens, or perhaps three fates, who seem to disrupt their peace, though the seer does not go

---

[1] 'Voluspo', in *The Poetic Edda*, trans. by Henry Adams Bellows (Princeton: Princeton University Press, 1936), pp. 1–27 (p. 4).

[2] *Ibid.*, pp. 4–5.

into detail. Then comes the creation of the dwarves by the gods. Tolkien borrows the names of Gandalf and most of the 13 dwarves in *The Hobbit* from the catalogue of dwarves in Völuspá. The seer then briefly describes the creation of human beings, Ask and Embla, the first man and woman, who were formed from two trees. To their lifeless bodies, Odin gave soul; Honir gave them sense; Loki gave them heat and hue.

There are a few similarities between the creation account of Völuspá and that of *The Silmarillion*. The world is not eternal but created. There is a primeval void before the creation of the world. The world is fashioned by gods in Völuspá and by the Ainur in *The Silmarillion*. The world began as good in both. In Völuspá, the gods war with giants, bringing about chaos and destruction and lasting enmity that affects both gods and men. In *The Silmarillion*, Melkor disrupts Ilúvatar's good creation and wars against the other Ainur, bringing world-shattering destruction to Arda, and later to the Children of Ilúvatar, Men and Elves.

There are many differences between Völuspá and *The Silmarillion*. There is no music in Völuspá. Völuspá does not tell how Ymir the giant came to be, nor how the gods came to be. It is not creation ex nihilo; the world is formed from Ymir's body. *The Silmarillion* tells of Ilúvatar, who is the only true god, who alone can create ex nihilo and who created all the Ainur. The Ainur aid him or, in the case of Melkor, attempt to thwart his harmony. There is one god in *The Silmarillion* and one chief source of evil, Melkor; whereas there are many gods and giants in Völuspá. Creation in Völuspá is from an act of the gods, forming earth, sea, and heaven from Ymir's flesh and blood. *Silmarillion* creation is by the word and by music. Motives are unclear as to why the gods in Völuspá fashion the earth. Ilúvatar's motives in creation also are not completely clear, but he creates freely, and his Ainur and their free music makes him glad. Perhaps that is reason enough to create. Ilúvatar says:

> Of the theme that I have declared to you, I will now that ye make in harmony together a Great Music. And since I have kindled you with the Flame Imperishable, ye shall show forth your powers in adorning this theme, each with his own thoughts and devices, if he will. But I will sit and hearken, and be glad that through you great beauty has been wakened into song (*Silmarillion*, p. 15).

The Kalevala is a Finnish epic compiled by Elias Lönnrot and originally published in 1835. Tolkien read and enjoyed the Kalevala and it provided him with inspiration for some of his own works. Túrin Turambar resembles Kullervo, and Sauron's ring bears similarities to the Sampo. The Kalevala, like all epic myths, has a creation story. It begins with the sky goddess Ilmatar, daughter of the Ether, leaving heaven to dwell by the ocean. Impregnated by the ocean, she becomes heavy and can no longer return to the sky but must remain in the water. A duck flies over Ilmatar, looking for ground to build a nest. Taking pity on the duck, Ilmatar raises her knees above the water, and on her knees the duck nests and lays seven eggs. Before the eggs hatch, however, Ilmatar becomes hot from the sun and stirs, causing the eggs to fall into the sea. These are no ordinary eggs, however; they are not destroyed and lost in the water. Rather, they come together into two great pieces, one forming the earth and one forming heaven. From the white of the eggs come moonbeams, from the yellow comes sunshine. Ilmatar then begins her creation:

> Where her hand she turned in water,
> There arose a fertile hillock;
> Wheresoe'er her foot she rested,
> There she made a hole for fishes;
> Where she dived beneath the waters,
> Fell the many deeps of ocean;
> Where upon her side she turned her,
> There the level banks have risen[3]

Ilmatar's second creation, for whom she laboured for seven hundred years, is Vainamoinen, who is called 'the singer'. Vainamoinen, whose mother was the sky goddess Ilmatar and whose father was the sea, sows plants and asks birds to sing. To help his plants grow, Vainamoinen prays to Ukko, father of heaven, who is most likely the father of Ilmatar as well. Ukko bears some resemblance to Tolkien's Ilúvatar. Vainamoinen sings many songs, songs of heroes and legends of creation. He is challenged by Youkahainen, a talented singer and wizard from the 'dismal Northland'. Youkahainen had heard of the great songs of Vainamoinen, how he was a better singer than Youkahainen. Hearing this, the young wizard grew envious and angry and, ignoring the counsel of his mother and father, challenges Vainamoinen to a contest. Youkahainen boasts of his wisdom and skill, even saying that he knows how the world was created because he was there. Upon hearing this, Vainamoinen, old and wise, calls Youkahainen 'prince of liars'.[4]

---

[3] *The Kalevala*, trans. by John Martin Crawford, 3rd edn, 2 vols (Cincinnati: The Robert Blake Company, 1910), I, p. 10.
[4] *Ibid.*, p. 35.

In the fascinating creation story in the Kalevala, there is a creation by birth, as Ilmatar gives birth to the first man, and from the eggs of the duck come the material Ilmatar uses to fashion the earth. *The Silmarillion* creation is not creation by birth. There is, however, an ancient singer and sower of plants, Vainamoinen, like the ancient Ainur sing and sow plants in Arda. Another similarity between the Kalevala and *The Silmarillion* is that Ukko seems to be the one God, father of all, like Ilúvatar is all-father. The singing contest between Vainamoinen and Youkahainen can also be likened to Melkor's disruption of the musical theme of Ilúvatar, though the consequences of Melkor's discord are far more disastrous. Youkahainen and Melkor are both princes of liars.

The Kalevala does not explain many things, such as how humans were created. It describes the parentage of Vainamoinen but no other humans. It does not say how Ilmatar is created or how the duck is created, or the sea or the sun. The Kalevala does not explain the presence of evil in the world. *The Silmarillion* creation account describes how Melkor's pride and envy are the initial sins, from which spring disobedience and later violence, as he attempts to mar and destroy the creation of Ilúvatar and the works of the Ainur, ultimately resulting in suffering and death for untold numbers of the Children of Ilúvatar.

Having examined the creation accounts of Völuspá and the Kalevala, the next theory is more philosophical than mythical; it is the Harmony of the Spheres. Around 500 BC, the Greek philosopher and mathematician Pythagoras suggested that the sun, moon and planets each emit a unique hum based on their orbital revolution, and that the quality of life on earth depends on the tenor of celestial sounds imperceptible to the human ear. Thus, the celestial bodies emit different notes based on their different sizes and rotations, and together they form a cosmic harmony. This is not creation by music *a la The Silmarillion*, but it is a heavenly symphony that, though it remains unheard by human ears, nonetheless affects life on earth. The Christian philosophers St Augustine and Boethius, who would have been well-known to Tolkien, took up the Pythagorean notion of the music of the spheres. St Augustine compared god's creation of the universe with that of a song-writer. Leo Spitzer discusses this in his book *Classical and Christian Ideas of World Harmony*. For Augustine, creation is a 'hymn scanned by God' and a 'poem of the world' which 'like any poem, can only be understood in time by a soul which endeavors to understand the action of Providence, which itself unfolds in time […] The God-Artist, creating in time, realizes his idea, his providential decisions, like a musician […]'.[5]

Another Christian philosopher, Boethius, in his treatise *De Institutione Musica* discusses three types of music: music of the spheres, harmony of human body and spiritual harmony, instrumental music. Through Augustine and Boethius, Pythagoras's philosophy of the Harmony of the Spheres spread throughout western thought and was influential during the middle ages and the renaissance. Robert R. Reilly discusses the power of philosophy:

> Philosophical propositions have a very direct and profound impact upon composers and what they do. John Adams, one of the most popular American composers today, said that he had 'learned in college that tonality died somewhere around the time that Nietzsche's God died, and I believed it.'

[5] Leo Spitzer, *Classical and Christian Ideas of World Harmony* (Baltimore: Johns Hopkins Press, 1963), p. 31.

The connection is quite compelling. At the same time God disappears, so does the intelligible order in creation. If there is no God, Nature no longer serves as a reflection of its Creator. If you lose the Logos of St. Clement, you also lose the ratio (logos) of Pythagoras. Nature is stripped of its normative power.[6]

Beginning with Pythagoras and continued and Christianized by St Augustine and Boethius, the concept of the Harmony of the Spheres, though not a creation story, may well have inspired the musical creation account of *The Silmarillion*.

It is time to turn to one of Tolkien's greatest inspirations: the book of Genesis. Tolkien was a devout Catholic and said that 'The Lord of the Rings is of course a fundamentally religious and Catholic work' (Letters, p. 172). If *The Lord of the Rings*, so too *The Silmarillion* is a Catholic work. The Genesis account is familiar, even to non-Christians:

> In the beginning God created the heavens and the earth. Now the earth was formless and empty, darkness was over the surface of the deep, and the Spirit of God was hovering over the waters. And God said, 'Let there be light,' and there was light. God saw that the light was good, and he separated the light from the darkness.[7]

Genesis describes one all-powerful god. Of his beginning, there is no account, for he is uncreated and eternal. He creates everything by the power of his word. *The Catechism of the Catholic Church* says:

---

[6] Robert R. Reilly, 'The Music of the Spheres, or the Metaphysics of Music', *Intercollegiate Review*, 37 (2001), 12–21 (p. 15).

[7] Genesis 1. 1-4.

Nothing exists that does not owe its existence to God the Creator. the world began when God's word drew it out of nothingness; all existent beings, all of nature, and all human history are rooted in this primordial event, the very genesis by which the world was constituted and time begun.[8]

The Catechism also says:

'In the beginning God created the heavens and the earth': three things are affirmed in these first words of Scripture: the eternal God gave a beginning to all that exists outside of himself; he alone is Creator […] the totality of what exists (expressed by the formula 'the heavens and the earth') depends on the One who gives it being.[9]

God, who needs nothing, gives existence to everything in the world. From his goodness and love, the world flows. He speaks and light appears for the very first time. He creates the sun, the moon and stars, the land and the seas, the plants and animals. Then god said, 'Let us make man in our image, after our likeness.' And so the child of god, man, was made with an immortal soul, with the power of rationality and free will to choose god or not, to serve god or to serve himself. God made the world good, but when Adam and Eve sinned, evil entered the world and with it, death.

Genesis, unlike *The Silmarillion*, does not speak of creation through music, and though it tells of angels and Satan the tempter, Genesis makes no mention of the angels singing with

---

[8] *Catechism of the Catholic Church*, 2nd edn (Vatican City: Libreria Editrice Vaticana, 1997), para. 338.

[9] *Ibid.*, para. 290.

god and helping to form and order the world. Nonetheless, Ilúvatar is very much like the god of Genesis. *The Silmarillion* opens with these words: 'There was Eru, the One, who in Arda is called Ilúvatar' (*Silmarillion*, p. 15). Ilúvatar is eternal; before creation, there is nothing but him. He is the source of all being. *The Silmarillion* continues, 'he made first the Ainur, the Holy Ones, that were the offspring of his thought, and they were with him before aught else was made. And he spoke to them, propounding to them themes of music; and they sang before him, and he was glad' (*Silmarillion*, p. 15). Ilúvatar is all-powerful; he has but to think of the Ainur, to will them into existence. He is the ultimate source of the Music. He gives the Ainur free will to sing in harmony with his great theme or not, as *The Silmarillion* says, 'ye shall show forth your powers in adorning this theme, each with his own thoughts and devices, if he will' (*Silmarillion*, p. 15). Ilúvatar is good and all of his creation is good. Melkor, because he is free, introduces discord into the Music; 'it came into the heart of Melkor to interweave matters of his own imagining that were not in accord with the theme of Ilúvatar; for he sought therein to increase the power and glory of the part assigned to himself' (*Silmarillion*, p. 16). From this initial discord in the Music, comes all the evil, suffering, and death with which Arda and the Children of Ilúvatar are burdened. Ilúvatar's Music, however, cannot be overcome. Melkor's music attempts to drown Ilúvatar's music 'by the violence of its voice, but it seemed that its most triumphant notes were taken by the other and woven into its own solemn pattern' (*Silmarillion*, p. 17). Thus, even discordant notes can be used in the divine harmony. So Ilúvatar explains to the Vala Ulmo, Lord of Water, how Melkor:

hath bethought him of bitter cold immoderate, and yet hath not destroyed the beauty of thy fountains, nor of thy clear pools. Behold the snow, and the cunning work of frost! Melkor hath devised heats and fire without restraint, and hath not dried up thy desire nor utterly quelled the music of the sea. Behold rather the height and glory of the clouds, and the everchanging mists; and listen to the fall of the rain upon the Earth! (*Silmarillion*, p. 19)

So from Melkor's cold and fire, against his own design, but according to the design of Ilúvatar, comes the beauty of snow and rain. Even death, perhaps the greatest evil on Arda that resulted from Melkor's discord, can be taken up into the Great Music of Ilúvatar. For, unlike the Elves, Men are mortal. Death, though it later was called the Doom of Man, was first the Gift of Ilúvatar to Man, that they should not dwell forever in Middle-earth, a land of shadows by the work of Melkor and his servants, but rather that Man may die and leave the earth and its sorrows behind. When Men fell under the shadow of Melkor, death became a grief to them because 'it seemed to them that they were surrounded by a great darkness, of which they were afraid' (*Silmarillion*, p. 265). Death is the great unknown, but it began as the Gift of Ilúvatar, and since all things were created by Ilúvatar, to him all things return. Not only Elves, but Men are the Children of Ilúvatar, so if they live by his word, then he is their hope, and death is but the gateway to never-ending life in Ilúvatar's home. As Aragorn son of Arathorn said at the end of his long life, 'In sorrow we must go, but not in despair. Behold! we are not bound forever to the circles of the world, and beyond them is more than memory. Farewell!' (*RK*, Appendix A, I, v).

Works Consulted

Bellows, Henry Adams, trans., *The Poetic Edda* (Princeton: Princeton University Press, 1936)

Catechism of the Catholic Church, 2nd edn (Vatican City: Libreria Editrice Vaticana, 1997)

Crawford, John Martin, trans., *The Kalevala*, 3rd edn, 2 vols (Cincinnati: The Robert Blake Company, 1910)

Reilly, Robert R., 'The Music of the Spheres, or the Metaphysics of Music', *Intercollegiate Review*, 37 (2001), 12–21

Spitzer, Leo, *Classical and Christian Ideas of World Harmony* (Baltimore: Johns Hopkins Press, 1963)

Transmission: an escape from death in Tolkien's work?

Gaëlle Abaléa

In *The Silmarillion*'s 'Ainulindalë' death is referred to as the Gift of Ilúvatar. Mortal men nonetheless tend to try and work their way around it, being jealous of the Elves who seem to have ended up with the better half of the bargain. Now, this attempt is probably in the nature of mortal humans. However, Tolkien tried to find a way to show that we could renounce this instinct and accept death as the gift it really is. Asli Bülbül Candaş develops in her paper, the Elves perspective, I will focus on Men's perspective and not mention the Elvish view on death nor their position or role in transmission. First, I'll examine Tolkien's many descriptions of the longing for eternal physical life, caused by the fear of the shadow of death and, taking many forms in Tolkien's work. I wish to show that, on the contrary, obtaining immortality through memory and transmission, which would explain the incredible number of genealogical trees in the legendarium and the symbolic of the tree itself, could appear a better way. Indeed, as a father, a teacher, a philologist and an artist Tolkien analysed through different works and characters the consequences both of transmission and the lack of transmission. The relationship between different generations, especially in time of conflict, is developed both through his most famous works as well as writings known mainly by fans and specialists. The artistic creation is also scrutinized as a means of transmission conducting to the immortality of the subject or the author sometimes of both. Many characters mention the possibility of being the heroes of song. In *Leaf by Niggle*, Tolkien also peeps into the world of the dead to glimpse on the surviving of artistic endeavour again using the symbol of a tree. However, even in the act of sub-creation, the shadow of pride might taint the wish for transmitting one's thought.

The longing for eternal physical life, caused by the fear of the shadow of death

The longing to escape death is central in Tolkien's work not only in the legendarium but also in almost all his works (apart maybe for the). The most evident example is probably the tale of the fall of Númenor told in the 'Akallabêth' in *The Silmarillion*. The estrangement of the Men of Númenor from the Elves of the Undying Land lies only in the fear of their own mortality and the jealousy they feel for the immortal elves. Two feelings resulting from Sauron's insidious counsel to King Ar-Pharazôn. The fact the rebellion of the people of Númenor is the result of the influence of Sauron shows Tolkien's feelings concerning the rejection of the wisdom the Eldar have tried to pass on to humans. This idea of death being the result of the perversion of evil is also developed in the 'Athrabeth Finrod ah Andreth' in *Morgoth's Ring* in which King Finrod Felagund discusses with a wisewoman named Andreth of the house of Bëor who reveals to him that Melkor has brought death on them. Andreth ascribes to Melkor powers only Eru is supposed to possess in the Elvish lore, thus, proving the terrible influence Melkor had on the spirit of Men. Hence, death is a subject of great fear in the heart of Men because it is linked to a shadow. When Finrod tries to point the difference between death and this shadow, Andreth answers in a mysterious and bitter tone about the Elvish incomprehension of human death.

This fear of death and longing for immortality is one of the reasons for the existence of the nine servants of the Ring. The characters of the Nazgûl illustrate perfectly the result of these artificially prolonged lives thanks to the power of the rings. The Nazgûl belong to neither the world of the living nor the world of the dead. The dread they inspire lies in the fact that their nature is unclear, they can no longer be referred to as humans but they belong to no other species. Gollum and Bilbo to a certain extend also show the reluctance Tolkien could feel about clinging to life beyond your time if not in as tragic a way as the Nazgûl. In all cases, though, the more they endure the less they look like their old selves. The longer they live, the less human they are. Gollum has lost his name like the Nazgûl who are only referred under that name and as a group. Maybe only the Witch-king keeps something like individuality. The longer they linger on, the longer the Ring gains power on them and seems to vampirize them and they lose everything that made them what they were. Therefore, they do not have anything to give or to pass on as they are only empty shells. Bilbo before parting definitely with the One Ring feels extremely tired: 'I feel thin, sort of stretched, like butter scraped over too much bread' (*FR*, I, i). We know he has changed forever, never really getting himself away from the fascination of the Ring.

On the contrary, Aragorn, after a long life, decides to leave the world (*RK*, Appendix A, I, v). He dies after fathering four children, and securing the future of Gondor and is one of the cornerstone of the lineage of the Kings of Gondor. Not only is he the fruit of the knowledge of the Eldar but he also passes on this knowledge to the next generation. This mission accomplished, he can welcome death serenely. The character of Aragorn is indeed linked to the theme of death as well as the theme of transmission being probably the most perfect embodiment of both. He himself has been taught in the way of his father and of the Eldar, both by his mother and by Elrond. So, the line has not been broken. This unbroken line of kings and Aragorn's fate is also linked to the White Tree of Gondor and the symbolism of the tree is paramount throughout Tolkien's work.

The symbolism of the tree

Indeed, who has never lost themselves in the wonderful and intricate lines of the numerous genealogic trees with the same name sprouting up every now and then, apparently parents giving to their children the name of an uncle or a grandmother to honour their memory. Of course, Tolkien did not invent the symbolism of the tree; however, he used it many times to express the passing of time, the succession of generations and the transmission of names, titles and characteristics.

In Tolkien's legendarium, this symbolism of the tree takes a mythical dimension. Telperion and Laurelin, the Trees of Valinor, especially after their destruction by Ungoliant, become the symbols of the light of the Valar, so the link to the Undying Land. When their light was captured inside the Silmarili, those jewels became subject to a fever both of reverence and madness. However, Yavanna gave a tree to the Elves similar to Telperion though it did not shine, called Galathilion. A sampling of it was passed on to the Eldar in Tol Eressëa. A sampling of Galathilion, Nimloth, was given to the Men of Númenor and was saved by Elendil and his followers who planted it in Gondor. In *The Return of the King*, when

Aragorn returns to Gondor, the tree blossoms again. This tree, the symbol of a long line of Men but also of the passing on of the knowledge from the Undying Land comes back to life when the alliance between the Eldar and the Edain is renewed with the heir of Isildur. So, generation after generation not only blood is passed through the line of Men but also a belief and a culture: the language of the Eldar and the resistance again to the power of Sauron. Therefore, even after the death of Elendil and the death of Isildur their beliefs and the reason for their deaths is remembered. This transmission allows at least a part of the dead ones, their belief, to endure even after their death through their followers.

The tragedy in Tolkien's work occurs when this transmission is made impossible. In the *Children of Húrin*, for example, the curse that Morgoth casts upon Húrin, is to witness the destruction of his own lineage victims of their own pride but also of misleading circumstances. However, in Húrin's case, the person who is supposed to transmit knowledge through advice is a prisoner of Morgoth. In other occurrences, this paternal figure is actually the cause of the severance of the lineage. Both Beorhtnoth and Thorin commit a fault or even a crime, Beorhtnoth out of pride Thorin out of greed, of sacrificing the young generation. The tragedy lies in the attitude of the youth who remain loyal to the figure of authority, and fight bravely and die doing their duty. So die the men of Beorhtnoth's *heorðwerod*, some of them his own relatives and so are slain Fíli and Kíli, Thorin's kinsmen fighting for Thorin thirst of gold and riches.

Now, Tolkien's experience as a young soldier who lost many of his friends on the battlefield may have influenced his writing of those characters. Elsewhere in this volume, Matthew

B. Rose depicts those dreadful months and I will not linger on it. What I feel is important is the pathos in the pages relating the passing of young people. However, if the passing of Théodred is lived by the different characters as a source of genuine sorrow, the transmission of the kingdom of Rohan to Éomer somewhat soften the blow. A parallel could be drawn with the *Fall of Arthur*, as Tânia Azevedo underlines in this volume, with the pity Arthur feels living his country unhealed, with no successor adding to the tragedy of the death of the king. Concerning Beorhtnoth and Thorin, the death of the youth in their family is lived as a real tragedy. Not only the chief is dead but the future generation who could have followed has been decimated. The line of transmission is cut hence not only individuals die but also all parts of knowledge, culture and memory.

Sub-creation

The decisions leading to such disastrous outcomes may come from a wish shared by many characters to become material for songs. Indeed, what a better way to make one's memory forever present after our death than being sung by poets and minstrels for everybody to hear for years on. Frodo and Sam discuss it on their way to Mordor, Éowyn mentions it when she realises that Aragorn will not return her love. In the *Homecoming of Beorhtnoth Beorthelm's Son*, Thorthelm and Tidwald, surrounded by maimed corpses on the battlefield in Maldon, remembers Finn, Froda and Horsa the heroes of stories of yore. Thorthelm being a minstrel's son has a rather chivalrous way of viewing the events he is part of, proving that century after their death, heroes are still remembered and also creating a terrible contrast between the reality of the battlefield and the way poets depicts it. It also creates a sort of irony, underlined by Tidwald, because hero or ordinary men, they all finish as a corpse on the battlefield. Of course, one could wonder whether it is really the memory of real men that still lives on through literature or a recreation of a vague memory that has become a reconstructed image. However, this chivalrous spirit, common to both Beorhtnoth and Beowulf, leads to very unwise decisions: Beorhtnoth decides to let the Vikings cross the bridge to appear fair and chivalrous putting his men's lives at risks in the doing. Likewise, Beowulf decides that he can take on the dragon on his own, risking his followers' life and also risking his country to be devastated, should he fail. Thus, the artistic creation of song and poems might somehow allow individuals or event to be remembered after they passed but the longing for this sort of immortality regardless of the consequences especially to others and especially to those we are responsible for, is not acceptable in Tolkien's eyes. And the memory will always be tainted somehow as with fault.

Nevertheless, artistic endeavour might still represent an acceptable way to escape oblivion seemingly promised by death. Tolkien's discuss this possibility in *Leaf by Niggle*, a very peculiar story in Tolkien's work though upon closer examination it can be seen as a rephrasing of many of Tolkien's favourite themes. At the core of the novel of course is the tree. The time-consuming tree which prevents Niggle from doing anything else though he has so many other tasks and duties to attend to. This tree might stands for artistic creation, at least the way Tolkien felt about it long before *The Lord of the Rings* was published, feeling already that he would never finish the great task of his mythology—a time consuming endeavour that takes over your life. It can seem useless to others but feel essential for

141

its creator as it makes him closer to the primeval act of creation and therefore to his own creator and at the same time serves as a legacy for future generations. Just like the genealogic tree symbolised a link between past, present and future, Niggle's tree can be seen as a metaphor of sub-creation using material that was already there, in the ground and expanding sky high for all to be seen. In the other world, Niggle is presented with his tree but there, it is achieved and presented as a part of vast landscape in which it is only a part as if sub-creation and artistic endeavour was a glimpse of the artist into the other world.

Conclusion

So, if we can claim that in Tolkien's mind death is not a curse but a gift and to try and escape death comes from a perversion of the intention of the creator, we could also balance the fact that transmitting a part of ourselves could be an acceptable way not to linger after our time but to live on through teaching and legacy. Like genetics which let parts of our ancestors live through us, the deeds, and reflexion of our dead, lives on through our actions and decisions. When we take the genealogic tree, with all those leaves representing many lives and we superpose them with the creative tree and the leaves symbolising the details of Tolkien's great work one could be stricken by the many lives Tolkien has deeply marked and the role his work has played for many people. Our being here together is certainly a proof that maybe transmission through artistic creation could be a way J.R.R Tolkien somehow cheated death.

Recurrent pattern of the Fall in Tolkien's legendarium

Massimiliano Izzo

Motivation

The kernel of this paper originates from a thread in Tolkien's thought that emerges from a variety of his writings—letters, essays, and commentaries—produced in the final years of the composition of *The Lord of the Rings* and those immediately after. This thread is best summarized by three key sentences that I will examine in a reversed chronological order. This procedure, I hope, provides a more convenient introduction to themes that are of crucial importance in Tolkien mythopoeic work. The first sentence, from a letter to Joanna de Bortadano, was written in 1956 after the publication of *The Lord of the Rings*, and reflects what Tolkien thought was the most important theme in his books:

> I do not think that even Power or Domination is the real centre of my story. […] The real theme for me is something much more permanent and difficult: Death and Immortality: the mystery of the love of the world in the hearts of a race 'doomed' to leave and seemingly to lose it; the anguish in the hearts of a race 'doomed' not to leave it, until its whole evil-aroused story is complete (*Letters*, p. 246).

This is a well-established concept and it is reformulated in nuanced forms, in two other letters of the same period, written to Herbert Schiro in 1957 (*Letters*, p. 262) and to Rhona Beare in 1958 (*Letters*, p. 284). A few years before, in 1951, when the novel was completed but the Professor was still struggling to find a publisher for both *The Lord of the Rings* and the 'Silmarillion', Tolkien wrote a seminal letter to the editor Milton Waldman where he outlined, in some ten thousand words, a full synopsis and the founding concepts of the whole legendarium. Together with the essay *On Fairy-stories*, it provides the best documentation of Tolkien's mythopoeic theory and the philosophy underlying his creative—or, in his own words, sub-creative—work. In this letter, before embarking in the description of the mythology Tolkien writes what in his opinion are the central themes of his mythology: 'Anyway all this stuff is mainly concerned with Fall, Mortality, and the Machine. With Fall inevitably, and that motive occurs in several modes' (*Letters*, p. 145). In this second sentence of the thread, Mortality—one of the two aspects of the Death/Immortality dichotomy—is connected with the Fall, the lapse from a state of grace to a state of sin, which is a central concept in Judaism and Christianity. A few lines below in the same paragraph Tolkien observes how in humans the sub-creative desire 'filled with the sense of mortality [...] has various opportunities of "Fall"' (*Letters*, p. 145). However, the opposite relation—i.e. seeing mortality as a consequence of the Fall of Man—is a central tenet of Christian, and in particular Catholic, doctrine.[1] So, it appears that the relationship between the two concepts goes both ways and I will illustrate how this cause-effect circularity, is also present, to some extent, in Tolkien's literary works. The possible ambiguity, as we will see, will be handled by Tolkien

---

[1] *Catechism of the Catholic Church*, 2nd edn (Vatican City: Libreria Editrice Vaticana, 1997), paras 400, 402, 403.

envisioning different traditions for the mortal (Men) and the immortal (Elves) species of the rational incarnates. This third sentence, the one at the beginning of the thread, was with any probability written sometime in 1944 when the Professor, having hit a halt in the composition of *The Lord of The Rings*, shifted his focus back to the core of his mythological work for a period of over one year. The quote is the very first sentence of the second draft of a sketchy document called 'The theory of this version': 'Evil reincarnates itself from time to time—reiterating, as it were, the Fall' (*Sauron*, p. 397). Some explanation is required here to clarify which version of what is Tolkien referring to in the title of the document. This document is one in a series of three sketches that provide the germ for a human centred ('mannish') version of the mythology, which up to that point—as *The Book of Lost Tales*, the 'Quenta Noldorinwa', and the 'Quenta Silmarillion'—had been wholly composed from an elvish perspective. This mannish version outlined in the sketches burgeoned into 'The Drowning of Anadûnê', an extended and more elaborated retelling of 'The Fall of Númenor'. The latter was originally composed in 1936 as a companion for the abandoned time-travel story 'The Lost Road'; in a similar way, 'The Drowning of Anadûnê' was written alongside 'The Notion Club Papers', ultimately abandoned in 1946. In this new creative effort, as stated by Christopher Tolkien, new ideas emerged, in particular concerning 'the shape of the world' and the 'Fall of Men' (*Sauron*, p. 405). In the light of this observation, the statement above, explicitly connecting for the first time the Fall to the recurrent incarnation of Evil (with any probability intended with a capital letter), acquires a major importance. It is at this point that explicitly emerges in Tolkien's writings the concept of the persistence

145

(seen as reincarnation, from a mythical point of view) of Evil, seen as strictly interconnected with a reiteration, or recurrence, of the Fall. Even though 'The Drowning of Anadûnê' and related sketches were not published until 1992 in *Sauron Defeated*, there is evidence that the concept of the recurrent nature of evil—frequently referred as the Shadow—bore great importance during the later revisions of the 'Silmarillion'.

The thread here evidenced connects in three key sentences Death (together with the dualism Mortality/Immortality), the Fall, and the recurrence of Evil. In this paper I propose to investigate the legendarium by exploring whether the concept of the reiteration of the Fall can be highlighted in relation to the recurrence of a mythical manifestation of evil, and whether it is possible to pin down recurrent patterns in the Fall, examining the different rational creatures that populate Tolkien's universe.

The beginning of evil

The origin of evil, authored by Melkor, is described in the 'Ainulindalë'. Desiring to 'bring into Being things of his own' (*Morgoth*, p. 9), he introduces discord in the music that his brethren, the Ainur, are playing under the Theme of Eru Ilúvatar, the sole god.

> 'Evil', in the arrogance and egotism of Melkor, had already appeared in the first attempts of the Spirits to express the Design of Eru communicated to them only in pure direct 'thought'. This was represented as taking the form of music: the Music of the Ainur (Holy Ones). In this Melkor, and those influenced by him, had introduced things of Melkor's own

146

thought and design, causing great discords and confusion.[2]

It is notable that, with the exception of *The Book of the Lost Tales*, Tolkien never uses the capital word Evil in his fiction, while it appears from time to time in his letters, commentaries, and linguistic writings. Evil is in its origin discord introduced in the harmony of the Design of Eru, and the capital word Evil in Tolkien's writings refers to a supernatural or demonic manifestation of evil in analogous to the Christian devil. When personified, Evil always refers to either Melkor (*Letters*, pp. 146, 148; *Sauron*, p. 401; *Morgoth*, pp. 330, 334) or Sauron (*Letters*, pp. 151, 154, 160, 190, 207, 252; *Sauron*, pp. 403–04). The Great Music of the Ainur is, borrowing the term from Flieger,[3] the 'blueprint' for Eä, the World that Is, the created Universe. So the discord generated by Melkor in the Music introduces the potency of the Fall in Eä. This primeval Fall happens outside Time, and outside the World; it will not recur but will provide the ontological basis for any fall that will happen within Eä (*Letters*, pp. 286–87).

A hierarchy of beings, a hierarchy of Evil

The world of the legendarium is inherently hierarchical. This is an established concept in Tolkien scholarship, well exposed by Dimitra Fimi mostly from an anthropological point of view and by Jonathan McIntosh in the framework of Thomistic

---

[2] J.R.R. Tolkien, 'Words, Phrases and Passages in various tongues in The Lord of the Rings', ed. by Christopher Gilson, *Parma Eldalamberon*, 17 (2007), 11–219 (p. 178).

[3] Verlyn Flieger, *Splintered Light: Logos and Language in Tolkien's Work*, 2nd edn (Kent: The Kent State University Press, 2012), p. 58.

philosophy.[4] McIntosh argues that Tolkien presents a hierarchy of diverse and unequal beings. Their different nature provides each category of beings with its own peculiar tendency to evil, insofar an individual fails to achieve the 'natural' level of goodness of its own category. The peculiar tendency towards evil will result in a peculiar modality of fall:

> Tolkien is careful to depict his characters as tending towards a form of evil unique to the nature of the particular species to which the character belongs and therefore to the particular ways in which that species can fail to realize its true being.[5]

There are three orders of beings that are of relevance in the legendarium from a metaphysical point of view: Ainur, Elves (Quendi), and Men (Atani). Each of them is different and fulfils a specific role within the mythology. The Ainur, 'the offsprings of Eru's thought' (*Morgoth*, p. 8), are 'divine' in the sense that their creation precedes the conception of the Universe and that they participate in its creation through the Music (*Letters*, p. 146). Those of them who enter Eä are bound to it until its uttermost end (*Morgoth*, p. 14). By their nature they are pure spirits, but they can assume a material appearance, though their body is more akin to a raiment, and they can be discarded at their pleasure. Their role is first sub-creative during the music, and afterwards 'demiurgic' (*Morgoth*, p. 330) during the early stages of preparation of the coming of the other two orders of beings, collectively called 'The Children of Ilúvatar'. The

---

[4] Dimitra Fimi, *Tolkien, Race and Cultural History: From Fairies to Hobbits* (London: Palgrave Macmillan, 2010), pp. 141–51.

[5] Jonathan S. McIntosh, *The Flame imperishable: Tolkien, St. Thomas, and the Metaphysics of Faërie* (Ann Arbor: ProQuest, 2009), p. 335.

role of the most powerful among them, the Valar, is to rule, specifically in relation to their sphere of competence, in accord with the will of their creator. The other two kinds are 'evidently in biological terms one race' (*Letters*, p. 189), but they are far different in metaphysical terms. Both kinds are incarnated rational beings—Mirröanwi in Quenya—constituted of two parts: hröa, a material body, and fëa, that can roughly be assimilated to the soul and proceeds directly from Eru, outside Eä, at the moment of conception (*Morgoth*, p. 336). This common dual nature notwithstanding, Elves are immortal or, in the words of Tolkien, enjoy a serial longevity. Moreover, they are bound to the word (in their case Arda, the Earth) until its end: if killed, by deadly wound or grief, their fëa remains in Arda and is summoned to the Halls of Mandos, for a period of healing and to be examined for possible reincarnation. In these two aspects Elves are closer to the Ainur than to Men (and possibly all the non-rational incarnates, that do not seem to enjoy everlasting life). Indeed, the role of the Elves is mostly sub-creative, mirroring in this the Ainur during the Music, and artistic. Their doom is 'to love the beauty of the world' and 'to bring it to full flower with their gifts of delicacy and perfection' (*Letters*, p. 147). Men on the other hand are mortal, in the sense that they are short-lived and not bound to the World, and therefore to Time. When death comes their fëa departs, leaving the body behind. Death is seen as 'gift' given to Men by Eru himself in the 'Silmarillion', which was originally conceived as written from the elvish perspective. However, in some writings drawing from the mannish tradition this concept is challenged, at least in some respect. More of this will be discussed in the following content.

149

The first pattern: the Fall of the Ainur

The recurrent unit consists of full cycle of three 'Falls', involving in turn each of the three orders of beings. The first step is the Fall of a powerful Ainu. He will start from a positive desire—or Melkor a sub-creative desire, for Sauron a desire for order and effectiveness—that will provoke a gradual fall into Domination. Tolkien states this explicitly in the letter to Milton Waldman: '[the Enemy] in successive forms is always "naturally" concerned with sheer Domination, and so the Lord of magic and machines' (*Letters*, p. 146). The fallen Ainu becomes the mythical manifestation of Evil for that Age of the World. He is described in Tolkien's letters as 'the Power of Evil visibly incarnate' (*Letters*, p. 148), the 'visible incarnation of Evil' (*Letters*, p. 157), and 'an evil daemon incarnated as a physical enemy' (*Letters*, p. 207), stressing his supernatural nature. He assumes the role of the 'Enemy', analogous to the one of Satan in the Christian tradition. He will thus proceed to mar the creation of his god and corrupting his children, inducing their subsequent fall into evil, and bringing a full cycle of Falls to completion.

Though the first sub-creative Fall of Melkor happens before the creation of Eä, its becoming evil begins only in the making of the Earth, during the very first days of Arda:

> NB Melkor (inside Eä) only really becomes evil after the achievement of Eä in which he played a great and powerful part (and in its early stages in accord with the fundamental Design of Eru). It was jealousy of Manwë and desire to dominate the Eruhín that drove him mad.[6]

---

[6] J.R.R. Tolkien, 'Fragments on elvish reincarnation', in *J.R.R. Tolkien,*

In the 'Ainulindalë' it is related how, since the early stages of Arda, Melkor aspires after its overlordship: 'When therefore Earth was young and full of flame Melkor coveted it, and he said to the Valar: 'This shall be my own kingdom! And I name it unto myself!'' (*Morgoth*, p. 14). The 'Ainulindalë' is a legend of Elvish origin, originally composed by Rúmil of Túna and narrated by Pengolodh the sage to Ælfwine (*Morgoth*, p. 8). A similar statement can be found in the mannish 'The Drowning of Anadûnê' where the reference to the (satanic) rebellion of Melkor against the creator is even more explicit: 'But it is said that long ago, even in the making of the Earth, the Lord Arûn [Melkor] turned to evil and became a rebel against Êru, desiring the whole world for his own and to have none above him' (*Sauron*, p. 357). Just as the rebellion to Eru's themes brought discord into the music played by the Ainur, so the desire of Melkor to become lord and king of the world brings discord and strife between him and the Valar with great turmoil in the early days of Arda. Many representations of harmony will be broken as a consequence of Melkor's actions and of his war against the other powers. The lamps, the primeval vessel of the unsullied light will be destroyed and the symmetry of Arda will be broken in their collapse together with the original abode of the Valar, the isle of Almaren. Even before the overthrow of the lamps, Melkor starts the marring, or corruption of Arda, that will be brought forth when the Valar are forced to abandon Middle-earth and retire into Aman, surrendering de facto the control of Middle-earth to their enemy.

The whole activity of Melkor on Earth is described by

---

l'effigie des Elfes, ed. by Michaël Devaux, *La Feuille de la Compagnie*, 3 (Paris: Bragelonne, 2014), pp. 94–159 (p. 152).

Tolkien in the post-1950 'Silmarillion' with the term 'marring of Arda'. This concept, together with the identification of Melkor as 'the Marrer' (i.e. the author of the marring), becomes of central importance in all the subsequent writings. Sainton has exposed how the term 'marring' conveys the multiple meanings of opposition (to Eru's design), damage/despoilment/ruin (of the world), and of affliction (of all the living creatures).[7] Only after the awakening of the Elves do the Valar bring war against Melkor, destroy his fortress Utumno, and carry him to Aman as a captive. However, it is already too late to heal the marring: many of his servants and the evils he has bred hide in the dark places of the Earth, waiting for the return of their master. In order to protect the Elves from these perils, the Valar invite them to Aman. The consequence will be the sundering of the different tribes of the Elves during the long march to the West, an event that will create the first disharmony among the Firstborn. Moreover, it is stated that, as a consequence of the marring of Arda, the Elves will come to first know death, the severance of fëa and hröa, and the fading of their bodies consumed by long ages of deathlessness (*Morgoth*, p. 56). Only after over four centuries of war and further evil against the Valar and the children of Eru, Melkor, now become Morgoth the Black Foe, is defeated and expelled from the world. However, his evil lingers in Arda once more, waiting for a new manifestation of darkness to arise and a new cycle in the iteration of evil to begin. The suggestion is explicit in 'The Drowning of Anadûnê' and it is even suggested

---

[7] Jérôme Saiton, 'Le marrissement d'Arda: fil et traduction de la catastrophe du conte', in *J.R.R. Tolkien, l'effigie des Elfes*, ed. by Michaël Devaux, *La Feuille de la Compagnie*, 3 (Paris: Bragelonne, 2014), pp. 233–77 (pp. 246–59).

the possibility that the new embodiment of evil is actually a reincarnation of the previous one:

> But after an age, there arose a second manifestation of the power of darkness upon Earth: a new shape of the Ancient Shadow, it may be, or one of its servants that drew power from it and waxed strong and fell. (*Sauron*, p. 363, emended as per p. 388)

The ambiguity is removed in 'Of the Rings of Power and the Third Age' where it is explicitly stated the nature of the new incarnation of evil, once again a fallen Ainu, though of a lesser degree and power than Melkor: Sauron, a Maia who entered into Melkor's service even before the destruction of the lamps (*Morgoth*, p. 52). His desire, as it was for his former master, is to achieve domination over Middle-earth: 'But he [Sauron] ruled rather by force and fear, if they might avail; and those who perceived his shadow spreading over the world called him the Dark Lord and named him the Enemy.' (*Silmarillion*, p. 346). Once again, the recurrent theme of absolute domination is more explicit in 'The Drowning of Anadûnê': 'Yet it was the purpose of Zigûr [Sauron], as of Mulkhêr [Morgoth] before him, to make himself a king over all kings, and to be the god of Men.' (*Sauron*, p. 363). The theme of the usurpation of god's right might appear absent — as well as god — from *The Lord of Rings*, but Tolkien did consider it the nexus of the War of the Ring and possibly, by extension, of all the previous wars between the free people and the Dark Lords:

> In The Lord of the Rings the conflict is not basically about 'freedom', though that is naturally involved. It is about

God, and His sole right to divine honour. The Eldar and the Númenóreans believed in The One, the true God, and held worship of any other person an abomination. Sauron desired to be a God-King, and was held to be this by his servants if he had been victorious he would have demanded divine honour from all rational creatures and absolute temporal power over the whole world. (*Letters*, pp. 243–44)

Given that Sauron's motivations, unlike Melkor's, were not sub-creative at the beginning, he is content with dominating the wills of the other rational beings rather than the physical matter of Arda. However, the effect of his rule on his subjected lands is no less dismal than Melkor's as it can be attested by the descriptions of Mordor and its surroundings in *The Lord of the Rings*.

Both in Melkor's and Sauron's case, as the evil Ainu proceeds in his trajectory of Fall, he is able for a time to keep separate two aspects: the foul and terrific role of the Enemy and the fair countenance of the tempter. The latter he will use to deceive Elves and Men. This duality of aspects is explicitly observed by Tolkien for Sauron: 'Sauron endeavoured to keep distinct his two sides: enemy and tempter' (*UT*, p. 328). At a certain point, a 'catastrophic' and irreversible event will strip him of his fair hue, and he will be able to act only as an open Enemy. For Sauron this event is the Downfall of Númenor. For Morgoth a specific event is not stated explicitly but, according to the 'Silmarillion', it appears to be the destruction of the Two Trees. However, he might have maintained a residual capacity to wear a fair appearance until the first Fall of Men, if this happened subsequently (a subject which was open to revision in the later texts [*Morgoth*, pp. 378, 385 417, 423]).

154

The Second Pattern: the Fall of the Elves

The most common modality of Fall for the Elves is the consequence of a selfish love towards their own sub-creations: they desire to be the masters of their own sub-creations and, as a consequence, masters of their own fates. This weakness of the Elves is exploited by the Enemy. He induces them into rebellion—implicit or explicit—towards the Valar, the lawful authorities of the world. Being the Elves bound to Arda, their rebellion does not involve a rejection of Eru, nor an allegiance to the Enemy, who, once his malice is discovered, becomes their main adversary. The starting motive of the Elves is the preservation of something that risks being lost, but this rightful sentiment is soon perverted into possessiveness. At the same time, their inner art—what Tolkien refers in *On Fairy-stories* also as enchantment—is perverted to power, the actual alteration of the primary world. Power in Tolkien's writings is 'always used with a negative connotation when it is not referred to one of the Valar' (*Letters*, p. 152).

In their first Fall, the Elves are deceived by Melkor, freed after three ages of imprisonment, wearing his fair countenance. Only a specific minority of the Elves are deceived. A recurring pattern here is that the wisest among them, the ones who are both physically and spiritually closer to the light and to the Valar do not trust Melkor to begin with. The ones that he lures, are those more invested in gathering knowledge, that at times is even referred as 'hidden knowledge':

> The Vanyar held him in suspicion [...], and to the Teleri he gave little heed [...]. But the Noldor took delight in the hidden knowledge that he could reveal to them; and some hearkened

to words that it would have been better for them never to have heard. (*Morgoth*, p. 274)

These Noldor listen to Melkor and are slowly but inexorably swayed by his lies. They start to think about returning to Middle-earth and to have there their own kingdoms, more beautiful and free than Aman itself:

> Visions he would conjure up in their hearts of the mighty realms that they could have ruled at their own will, in power and freedom in the East; and then whispers went abroad that the Valar had brought the Eldar to Aman because of their jealousy, fearing that the beauty of the Quendi and the makers' power that Ilúvatar had bequeathed to them would grow too great for the Valar to govern, as the Elvenfolk waxed and spread over the wide lands of the world. (*Morgoth*, p. 275)

The consequences are, as in the case of the previous rebellions of Melkor, discord and the disruption of previous harmony. Unrest and discontent poison the peace of Valinor, strife stirs within the House of Finwë between his sons, the half-brothers Fëanor and Fingolfin. Fëanor, who made the Silmarils in foresight to preserve the light of the Two Trees, is increasingly consumed by his possessive desire towards them. Once Melkor destroys the Two Trees, the second and last vessels of the unsullied light, and steals the Silmarils, the harmony is irremediably lost: the consequences are the kinslaying at Alqualondë and the subsequent ban and curse on the Noldor. More tears, death, and suffering await the exiles in Beleriand and the rest of Middle-earth at the hands of Morgoth and his servants, and further strife and betrayal among Elves, until the bitter end of the First Age.

The fall of the Elves at the hands of Sauron in the Second Age is a minor one, and involves a small number of them; nonetheless its consequences are dire. Various patterns of the first one are repeated. Once again, the Enemy wears a fair appearance but the wisest and closest to the West—i.e. to the Valar—of the Elves of Middle-earth do not trust him: 'to Lindon he did not come, for Gil-galad and Elrond doubted him and his fair-seeming' (*Silmarillion*, p. 344). Once again, the Elves more interested in craft and knowledge listen to the Enemy:

> It was in Eregion that the counsels of Sauron were most gladly received, for in that land the Noldor desired ever to increase the subtlety of their works [...]. Therefore they hearkened to Sauron, and they learned of him many things, for his knowledge was great. (*Silmarillion*, p. 344)

Once again, they rebel—though implicitly—to the authority of the Valar, as Tolkien observes in his letter to Milton Waldman: 'Sauron found their weak point in suggesting that, helping one another, they could make Western Middle-earth as beautiful as Valinor. It was really a veiled attack on the gods, an incitement to try and make a separate independent paradise' (*Letters*, p. 152). The consequences are the forging of the Rings of Power, and two ages of war in Middle-earth that will end only with the War of the Ring, and more losses and suffering for the few Elves that have not yet sailed to the West.

The metaphysics of the Faeries

In the light of what discussed in the previous two sections, it is useful to analyse the patterns of the Fall of the 'fantastic' (and immortal) beings of the legendarium, Ainur and Elves, in the light of Tolkien's theory of fantasy as laid down in *On Fairy-stories*. There, in the section aptly named 'Fantasy' (*TL*, pp. 53–54), the Professor describes a metaphysical framework for his secondary world based on various 'binary oppositions', to borrow the term used by the French philosopher Jacques Derrida in his critics of structuralism and, more in general, of western metaphysics.[8] The concept of sub-creation is opposed to domination, which is elsewhere defined as 'tyrannous re-forming of Creation' (*Letters*, p. 146), art and enchantment are opposed to power and magic (and the machine). Thirdly, the role of the sub-creator is opposed to the one of the magician. Many years later, in an essay written as a commentary on the novella *Smith of Wootton Major*, Tolkien drew the opposition between the 'love of Faery', seen as the 'love of love' (i.e. 'selfless love towards all things, animate and inanimate') and the impulse of possession and domination.[9] The metaphysical system outlined in *On Fairy-stories* is reiterated almost twenty years later. In general the duality is between creativity expressed as an internal, almost 'spiritual' quality and creativity exerted outside, to the damage and detriment of the primary world. In *On Fairy-stories* these oppositions are referred to the sub-creator in 'our' primary world, but they apply also to the 'Fairies', the inhabitants of Faërie, and therefore to Ainur and Elves in the universe of Eä. Those of them who fall into evil do

---

[8] See for instance: Jacques Derrida, 'Structure, sign, and play in the discourse of the human sciences', in her *Writing and Difference* (London: Routledge & Kegan Paul Ltd, 1978), pp. 351–70 (p. 357).

[9] J.R.R. Tolkien, *Smith of Wootton Major: Extended Edition*, ed. by Verlyn Flieger (London: HarperCollins, 2005), p. 101.

that along the lines drawn by the oppositions outlined above.

The Third Pattern: the Fall of the Men

What can be said about Men? Well, they constitute a different story altogether. As Tolkien stated in the letter to Milton Waldman, the original Fall of Men was due to appear off-stage in the legendarium, being the Silmarillion, at least in 1951 when the letter was written, elf-centred. This consideration notwithstanding, there exist at least two accounts of the first Fall of Men, told from the mannish perspective: a very short one, contained in the third paragraph of 'The Drowning of Anadûnê', and the full account of the 'Tale of Adanel'. The latter itself contained within the framework of the 'Athrabeth Finrod ah Andreth', the dialogue between the elven lord Finrod Felagund and Andreth, Wise-woman of the House of Bëor. The second Fall happens in the Second Age and culminates with the Downfall of Númenor whose final account is related in the homonymous tale, also known as the 'Akallabêth'. The pattern of the Fall for mankind works as follows. Men are tempted by the Enemy, who, as seen before, desires to become a god-king to them, and they are seduced into rejecting their nature and their privileged relationship with Eru. This rejection, or its direct consequences, will provoke a direct intervention of Eru in the world that will leave Men bereft of hope after death. This state of hopelessness and despair is referred by Tolkien as the 'Shadow of Death' (*Lost Road*, p. 47; *Sauron*, p. 247), which for Men is, as evidenced by Devaux, the shadow cast by the fear of death,[10] the fear of the unknown without any hope—

---

[10] Michäel Devaux, '"The Shadow of Death" in Tolkien', in *2001: A Tolkien*

symbolized by darkness—that awaits Men beyond the circles of the world.

In the main text of 'Athrabeth', the first Fall is only hinted. Finrod thinks that death is natural to Men, in the sense that is part of the original design of Eru for them. Andreth replies that this is not the case, arguing that the severance of fëa and hröa is unnatural and therefore evil, and was imposed on Men by the malice of Melkor, whom she names the Lord of this World. This title echoes the biblical *Princeps huius mundi*, as evidenced by Shippey.[11] Finrod denies that Melkor, however mightiest among the Ainur in the beginning, could have the power to change the fate of the children of Eru, a power that, according to him, belongs only to Eru himself. He agrees however that the severance of fëa and hröa is not natural, and hypothesizes that Men, in an unfallen state, were anyway fated to leave the world, possibly through assumption.[12] He deduces that they did something that angered Eru who changed their fate. 'Therefore I say to you, Andreth, what did ye do, ye Men, long ago in the dark? How did ye angered Eru?' asks Finrod (*Morgoth*, p. 313). According to the 'Athrabeth' main text, Andreth refuses to give an answer to one of the Elves. However, in the commentaries on the 'Athrabeth' it is reported the existence of alternative versions written under a Númenórean influence, that is more directly influenced by the Mannish perspective. In

---

Odyssey. Proceedings of Unquendor's Fourth Lustrum Conference, Brielle, The Netherlands, 9 June 2001, trans. by David Ledanois, ed. by Ron Pirson (Leiden: De Tolkienwinkel, 2002), pp. 1–46 (pp. 35–36).

[11] T.A. Shippey, *J.R.R. Tolkien: Author of the Century* (London: HarperCollins, 2001), p. 263.

[12] This is an analogy with the virgin Mary, whose 'unfallen' state is referred by Tolkien in the letter to Rhona Beare (*Letters*, pp. 212–17).

these accounts, Andreth, pressed by the Elven prince, provides various answers, the longest and more detailed of them being the 'Tale of Adanel'. Regardless of the details of these different accounts, the key point is that 'all agree, however, in making the cause of disaster the acceptance by Men of Melkor as King (or King and God)' (*Morgoth*, p. 344). This statement is in accord with the tale as related in 'The Drowning of Anadûnê', some fifteen years before:

At the appointed hour Men were born into the world, and they were called the Êru-hin, the children of God; but they came in a time of war and shadow, and they fell swiftly under the domination of Mulkhêr, and they served him. And he now came forth and appeared as a Great King and as a god; and his rule was evil, and his worship unclean, and Men were estranged from Êru and from his servants. (*Sauron*, p. 358, emended as per p. 387)

Once again, the consequence of the Fall is the disruption of previous harmony: between the fëa and the hröa of Men, if we are to believe the hypothesis of Finrod; and between Men and the rest of Creation, according to the 'Tale of Adanel':

Thereafter we were grievously afflicted, by weariness, and hunger, and sickness; and the Earth and all the things in it were against us. Fire and Water rebelled against us. The birds and beasts shunned us or, if they were strong assailed us. Plants gave us poison; and we feared the shadow under the trees. (*Morgoth*, p. 348)

In the Second Age, 1500 years after the forging of Rings of Power, the pattern of the Fall of Men repeats itself in many aspects. Here the Númenóreans, Men fallen but who repented and contributed to Morgoth's overthrow, are rewarded with a longer life and an island located in the proximities of Aman and the Immortal Lands, that they are forbidden to visit. They gradually turn back to evil, desiring to achieve immortality and murmuring against the prohibition of the Valar. Under Ar-Pharazôn, their last and most powerful king, they bring Sauron into submission, but the Maia, using his stronger power, sways them and turns them back once again to the open cult of the dark, and of Melkor its lord. When they set sail to the West to wage war against the Valar and the Elves in order to achieve immortal life, Eru intervenes directly and changes once again the fate of the World, provoking the Downfall of Númenor, the destruction of Ar-Pharazôn's army, and removing Aman from the Earth. The few faithful Númenóreans who survive the cataclysm calls themselves the exiles and are once again left bereft from grace under the shadow of death, without any visible earthly paradise left on Earth.

Death, Immortality and the Fall

It appears evident that the Fall of Men is different from and in many ways more tragic and ruinous than the one of the Elves, provoking changes in the nature of Man and the world. Individual Elves may be tempted by the Enemy but they never swear allegiance to him; conversely, Men are deceived as a whole—or in the great majority, as in the second Fall—and enter into service of the Enemy, rejecting Eru as the sole god. Tolkien emphasizes this difference in the 'Athrabeth' commentary:

Individual Elves might be seduced in a kind of minor 'Melkorism' desiring to be their own masters in Arda, and have things their own way, leading in extreme cases to rebellion; but not one has ever entered the service or allegiance of Melkor himself, nor ever denied the existence and supremacy of Eru. Some dreadful thing of this sort, Finrod guesses, Men must have done, as a whole; [...] (*Morgoth*, p. 334)

Why is there such a distinctive difference in the outcome and modality of the Fall for the two orders of Mirröanwi? It seems reasonable to hypothesize that this is somehow related to their ontological differences, in particular the different relation of their spirits with the 'world in time' (*Letters*, p. 236), and as consequence with death. In the light of this observation, a possible answer is found in the 'Athrabeth' itself:

But the Power of Melkor over material things was plainly vast. The whole of Arda (and indeed probably many other parts of Eä) had been marred by him. Melkor was not just a local Evil on Earth, nor a Guardian Angel of Earth who had gone wrong: he was the Spirit of Evil, arising even before the making of Eä. His attempt to dominate the structure of Eä, and of Arda in particular, and alter the designs of Eru (which governed all the operations of the faithful Valar), had introduced evil, or a tendency to aberration from the design, into all physical matter of Arda. It was for this reason, no doubt, that he had been totally successful with Men, but only partially so with Elves (who remained as a people 'unfallen') His power was wielded over matter, and through it. (*Morgoth*, p. 334)

Here there are two aspects to take into consideration. One is the 'global', rather than 'local', role of Melkor as the primary spirit of evil, a role that makes him a closer equivalent to the Christian Satan than the Bent One is in C.S. Lewis's 'Space Trilogy', even though there the Christian reference is made explicit. The second is the observation that Melkor's evil had a stronger power over the matter rather than the spirit, and that this is one of the reasons why he achieved a complete success and the total domination of Men. What does this mean? In the 'Athrabeth', Finrod says to Andreth that the Elves call Men 'Guests', temporary passengers in Arda (and Eä). This statement can also be found in the 'Ainulindalë': 'but the sons of Men die indeed, and leave the World (it is said); wherefore they are called the Guests, or the Strangers' (*Morgoth*, p. 37). There is evidence that this is a long-standing concept in Tolkien's mythology. In 'The Lost Road', Elendil says to his son Herendil: 'Do not the Firstborn call us the Guests?' (*Lost Road*, p. 66). The fëa of Men, not belonging and being bound to Eä, has a more limited control over matter than the one of the Elves. As a consequence, it is far easier for Melkor to succeed in his intent with beings possessing a weaker strength of will (i.e. control over their own bodies and pulses).

However, the explanation here suggested is not completely satisfying in the light of the unfallen Man free from death, as envisioned by Finrod in the 'Athrabeth'. Another possibility can be found examining the role of Men, within the mythology. McIntosh observes that the conception of two different orders of being at creation must be justified by the peculiar role that each of them must play in the great drama.[13] Fornet-Ponse stresses that the role of Men is mainly eschatological while the one of the Elves is mostly artistic: 'Men have an eschatological

---

[13] McIntosh, p. 61.

"future"—fairies/elves not'.[14] Statements supporting this view can be found both in the 'Athrabeth' (*Morgoth*, pp. 318–19) and in the sketches that precede 'The Drowning of Anadûnê': 'Men (the Followers or Second Kindred) came second, but it is guessed that in the first design of God they were destined (after tutelage) to take on the governance of all the Earth, and ultimately to become Valar, to "enrich Heaven", *Iluve*' (*Sauron*, p. 401). If Men were supposed to achieve the healing of Arda Marred and to enlarge the Music in order to 'surpass the Vision of the World' (*Morgoth*, p. 318) it makes sense that Melkor would devote a special effort to tempt them into his service. Besides the 'Athrabeth', there is evidence of this also in the 'Ainulindalë' (version D): 'For it seems to us that Men resemble Melkor more of all the Ainur, and yet he has ever feared and hated them, even those that served him' (*Morgoth*, pp. 36–37). The reason for Melkor's fear and hatred is nowhere explained; however, it might have feared that Men be able to fulfil their eschatological role, even in a fallen state. Among the fallen Man there are those who keep the 'Old Hope', as it is referred in the 'Athrabeth', which contains towards the end a surprisingly explicit reference to 'Eru himself entering into Arda' (*Morgoth*, p. 421). This intrusion, as pointed by Agøy, leaves a positive message regarding the end of history and the redemption of all things in Eä.[15]

---

[14] Thomas Fornet-Ponse, '"Strange and free": on some aspects of the nature of Elves and Men', *Tolkien Studies*, 7 (2010) 67–89 (p. 73).

[15] Nils Ivar Agøy, 'The fall and man's mortality: an investigation of some theological themes in J.R.R. Tolkien's "Athrabeth Finrod ah Andreth"', in *Tolkien and the Powers of his World, Proceedings of the Arda Symposium at the Second Northern Tolkien Festival, Oslo, August 1997*, ed. by Nils Ivar Agøy (Oslo: Arda Special, 1998), pp. 16–27 (pp. 24–26).

One might ask which of the two hypotheses discussed above is correct. Given that the legendarium contains different accounts written from the point of view of the two kindreds, it is fair to conclude that both contain a germ of truth. More objectively, they are both consistent with the secondary world, at the same time echoing themes familiar with the mythologies of the primary one. As Verlyn Flinger observed regarding the 'Athrabeth', leaving this riddle unsolved with the adoption of different traditions and accounts, Tolkien makes his imaginary world more realistic rather than less.[16]

Afterword

The patterns outlined here do not want to be by any means exhaustive or omni-comprehensive. Many of the creatures not treated above do not fit well, and there are other exceptions. I have not treated Dwarves, since they were not conceived in the Great Music and are not treated in detail in Tolkien's more philosophical work. It could be argued that their most common modality of fall is into greed, excessive desire to possess things, and in this their similarities with the Noldor are evidenced. But no story of a first Fall of Dwarves is reported. Another category of beings that is ignored is the Úmaiar, the lesser Ainur who turned into Melkor's service, the most notable of them being the Balrogs (*Morgoth*, p. 79). Their role is secondary to Melkor's and they never act outside his will. They are actually seen in some of Tolkien's writings part of Melkor's will dispersed,

[16] Verlyn Flieger, 'Whose myth is it?', in *Between Faith and Fiction: Tolkien and the Powers of his World, Proceedings of the Arda Symposium at the Second Northern Tolkien Festival, Oslo, August 1997*, ed. by Nils Ivar Agøy (Oslo: Arda Special, 1998), pp. 35–42 (pp. 41–42).

therefore without an identity of their own (*Morgoth*, p. 411). Sauron himself acts as an utterly faithful servant of Melkor until his master's ultimate defeat and extrusion from Arda. Their existence does not invalidate the pattern of the Fall of the Ainur outlined before. Ungoliant shows an agenda of her own, but there is no evidence of her being an Ainu, and her existence could be a consequence of the discord introduced by Melkor in the music, as it is speculated in some later, albeit not definitive, writings about the Orcs (*Morgoth*, pp. 405–06). In conclusion, the mythopoeic imagery of Tolkien's work resists the constriction of regular rules or patterns to fit all cases. They provide however an insightful guide for the events and order of beings most important for the metaphysics of Tolkien's secondary world.

Works Consulted

Agøy, Nils Ivar, 'The fall and man's mortality: an investigation of some theological themes in J.R.R. Tolkien's "Athrabeth Finrod ah Andreth"', in *Between Faith and Fiction: Tolkien and the Powers of his World, Proceedings of the Arda Symposium at the Second Northern Tolkien Festival, Oslo, August 1997*, ed. by Nils Ivar Agøy (Oslo: Arda Special, 1998), pp. 16–27

Catechism of the Catholic Church, 2nd edn (Vatican City: Libreria Editrice Vaticana, 1997)

Derrida, Jacques, 'Structure, sign, and play in the discourse of the human sciences', in her *Writing and Difference* (London: Routledge & Kegan Paul Ltd, 1978), pp. 351–70

Devaux, Michäel, '"The Shadow of Death" in Tolkien', in *2001: A Tolkien Odyssey. Proceedings of Unquendor's Fourth Lustrum Conference, Brielle, The Netherlands, 9 June 2001*, trans. by David Ledanois, ed. by Ron Pirson (Leiden: De Tolkienwinkel, 2002), pp. 1–46

Fimi, Dimitra, *Tolkien, Race and Cultural History: From Fairies to Hobbits* (London: Palgrave Macmillan, 2010)

Flieger, Verlyn, 'Whose myth is it?', in *Between Faith and Fiction: Tolkien and the Powers of his World, Proceedings of the Arda Symposium at the Second Northern Tolkien Festival, Oslo, August 1997*, ed. by Nils Ivar Agøy (Oslo: Arda Special, 1998), pp. 35–42

——, *Splintered Light: Logos and Language in Tolkien's Work*, 2nd edn (Kent: The Kent State University Press, 2012)

Fornet-Ponse, Thomas, '"Strange and free": on some aspects of the nature of Elves and Men', *Tolkien Studies*, 7 (2010) 67–89

McIntosh, Jonathan S., *The Flame imperishable: Tolkien, St. Thomas, and the Metaphysics of Faërie* (Ann Arbor: ProQuest, 2009)

Saiton, Jérôme, 'Le marrissement d'Arda: fil et traduction de la catastrophe du conte', in *J.R.R. Tolkien, l'effigie des Elfes*, ed. by Michaël Devaux, *La Feuille de la Compagnie*, 3 (Paris: Bragelonne, 2014), pp. 233–77

Shippey, T.A., *J.R.R. Tolkien: Author of the Century* (London: HarperCollins, 2001)

Tolkien, J.R.R., *Smith of Wootton Major: Extended Edition*, ed. by Verlyn Flieger (London: HarperCollins, 2005)

——, 'Words, Phrases and Passages in various tongues in The Lord of the Rings', ed. by Christopher Gilson, *Parma Eldalamberon*, 17 (2007), 11–219

——, 'Fragments on elvish reincarnation', in *J.R.R. Tolkien, l'effigie des Elfes*, ed. by Michaël Devaux, *La Feuille de la Compagnie*, 3 (Paris: Bragelonne, 2014), pp. 94–159

Frodo and Saruman: euformation, dysformation, and immortality in The Lord of the Rings

Adam B. Shaeffer

For years scholars and fans—not to mention Tolkien himself—have noted that *The Lord of the Rings* is saturated with J.R.R. Tolkien's moral and theological vision. This essay will explore his vision by reading *The Lord of the Rings* through the lens of spiritual formation to examine two of the potential spiritual ends possible for the characters living within Middle-earth. In order to do this, I will follow in his footsteps and coin my own terms to frame our discussion, so that just as he refers to eucatastrophe and dyscatastrophe in his essay 'On Fairy Stories,' I will refer to spiritual growth as *euformation* and spiritual corruption as *dysformation*. Focusing mostly on Saruman, I will explore how his unique dysformative journey is characterized by a qualified loss of immortality, from disembodied pure spirit as a Maia to beastliness and ultimately to nothingness. By contrast, Frodo, whose euformative story I will only briefly touch on, is characterized by the exercise of pity and because of the pity and mercy he extends to others, he is offered the closest thing a mortal can receive to immortality within Arda.[1]

---

[1] Let me make it clear that I am not claiming Frodo receives immortality by sailing West. Tolkien is clear that Frodo will still die (e.g. *Letters*, pp. 198–99, 328), but when the time comes he will be able to 'die at [his] own desire and of free will' (*Letters*, p. 411). The gift given to him is that which is given to the Númenóreans, the gift to lay down their lives at the time of their choosing and to freely 'give back the gift' (*RK*, Appendix A, I, v).

Saruman

But first, a little background: Tolkien's mythology operates in a structured manner akin to the medieval conception of the cosmos as a great chain of being with Eru, or god, at the top and the lowest creatures at the bottom.[2] Saruman is one of the Istari—five Maiar (lesser angelic beings filling the third place in the chain below Eru and the Valar) sent to Middle-earth to kindle the hearts of Elves and Men to withstand the corruption and evil of Sauron.[3] But they were not sent in their natural angelic forms; instead they came 'clad in bodies as of Men, real and not feigned, but subject to the fears and pains and weariness of earth, able to hunger and thirst and be slain' (*UT*, p. 389). They were sent as agents of euformative community to encourage the flourishing of all creatures opposed to Sauron. As one sent in this manner, Saruman enters Middle-earth uncorrupted and unseduced by evil, yet Tolkien notes that the Istari 'might [...] fall away from their purposes, and do evil, forgetting the good in the search for power to effect it' (*UT*, p.

[2] For some helpful discussions of this feature of Tolkien's legendarium see *J.R.R. Tolkien Encyclopedia: Scholarship and Critical Assessment,* ed. by Michael D.C. Drout (London: Routledge, 2007), pp. 271–72; Dimitra Fimi, *Tolkien, Race, and Cultural History: From Fairies to Hobbits* (Basingstoke: Palgrave Macmillan, 2009); and Rose A. Zimbardo, 'Moral Vision in The Lord of the Rings', in *Understanding The Lord of the Rings: The Best of Tolkien Criticism*, ed. by Rose A. Zimbardo and Neil D. Isaacs (Boston: Houghton Mifflin, 2004), pp. 68–75.

[3] The Istari 'came out of the Far West and were messengers sent to contest the power of Sauron, and to unite all those who had the will to resist him; but they were forbidden to match his power with power, or to seek to dominate Elves or Men by force and fear' (*RK*, Appendix B, The Third Age).

390).[4] 'To this evil Saruman succumb[s]' (*Letters*, p. 237), and well before the text introduces him he has become faithless. The only glimpse we are given of the creature he once was comes in Gandalf's return as Gandalf the White, or 'Saruman as he should have been' (*TT*, III, v). If we follow Gandalf from his return onward, witnessing his power to create euformative communities wherever he goes, we will see what Saruman was capable of before his fall; we will see the power his voice could have had to effect growth and ennoblement. In his four appearances in the text we see him descend the chain from Istari to Maia,[5] from Maia to Man, from Man to Orc, and from Orc to disembodied and rejected spirit.

While the first stage in his descent happens before we first meet him, the change is obvious when we encounter him in Gandalf's report to the Council of Elrond. He shares that when he arrived at the foot of Orthanc, Saruman called himself 'Saruman of Many Colours' (*FR*, II, ii). When Gandalf says that he likes white better Saruman replies, 'White cloth may be dyed. The white page can be overwritten; and the white light can be broken' (*FR*, II, ii). Gandalf's response is telling; he says 'In which case it is no longer white [...] And he that breaks a thing to find out what it is has left the path of wisdom' (*FR*, II, ii). This exchange reveals that Saruman has abdicated his position as an Istari in an attempt to become the master and

---

[4] The 'good' here referenced is not just the good end for which they were sent—to empower Elves and Men to resist the evil influence of Sauron—but also refers to the good of those they were to be in community with: the thriving and ennoblement of all.

[5] While this is not a true descent down the chain of being, we will characterize it as such since it is a change in his purpose for being in Middle-earth and entails a loss of his potential for good within the world.

ruler of Middle-earth. While his change is not necessarily one of form or substance, it is a change in *telos* and is only the first step on a slippery downward slope. In not just failing to serve, but refusing to serve, he has initiated a process of dysformation that will result in changes to his body and soul. This fall will become more pronounced as we proceed.

When the characters next encounter Saruman he still believes he is in authority because he does not know of Gandalf's new stature. This time, his dysformation reveals itself in the way he uses his voice as a weapon intended to break down the bonds of euformative community Gandalf has built. 'Having lost any devotion to other persons or causes' (*UT*, p. 413), Saruman uses his voice to engender the same loss in others. But the successive voices of Gimli and Éomer break the spell, revealing Saruman's true nature and causing him to temporarily lose control of his voice, leaving those previously enticed by it to '[shudder] at the hideous change' (*TT*, III, x). Saruman masters himself and gathers his power for one final attempt at domination and persuasion, but this time he aims higher: he aims for Gandalf. This final exercise of power offers an even clearer glimpse into this dysformative use of Saruman's voice:

[N]ow the spell was wholly different. They heard the gentle remonstrance of a kindly king with an erring but much-loved minister. *But they were shut out, listening at a door to words not meant for them: ill-mannered children or stupid servants* overhearing the elusive discourse of their elders, and wondering how it would affect their lot. Of loftier mould these two were made: reverend and wise. It was inevitable that they should make alliance. Gandalf would ascend into the tower, to discuss deep things beyond their comprehension in the high chambers of Orthanc. *The door would be closed, and they would be left outside*, dismissed to await allotted work or punishment. (*TT*, III, x, emphasis mine)

Where Gandalf's power and presence generate communities where people can be ennobled and grow into their true selves, Saruman's voice creates barriers and distinctions between people. Where Gandalf encourages fellowship, Saruman brings division. But then Gandalf laughs and informs Saruman of the change in their respective situations saying, 'I fear I am beyond your comprehension' (*TT*, III, x). Had Saruman not fallen so far, he would have seen what Gandalf has become, but his inability emphasizes the change in his nature. No mortals, not even the wisest in Middle-earth, can understand what Gandalf has become because they have no real context by which to understand.[6] That Saruman is incapable demonstrates that he has become no more than human, though his physical change awaits the scene's conclusion.

Yet Saruman is not beyond hope, and this is crucial. Even considering how debased and dysformed he has become, clemency is still available. The chance to enter into the life-giving, euformative community Gandalf establishes is on offer, but Saruman cannot bring himself to accept. When at last he speaks, his voice—once melodious, powerful, and sweet—has become 'shrill and cold' (*TT*, III, x). Pride and hatred have won their short-lived battle against uncertainty and guilt. Gandalf makes the offer a second time, extending to Saruman the chance to walk away a free man should he so choose, but

---

[6] Arguably, only Galadriel among all the inhabitants of Middle-earth could fathom the change in Gandalf since she alone has walked the shores of Valinor and lived among the Valar and Maiar.

Saruman refuses, scorning the offered forgiveness.[7]

So, at last, Gandalf exerts his power. This breaker of community, this sower of dysformative seeds, cannot be allowed to continue in this manner. Gandalf commands Saruman to return, and Saruman has no choice except to obey. He turns back, and 'as if dragged against his will' returns to the encounter (*TT*, III, x). Gandalf denounces Saruman, exposing his sin and folly for all to see:

> 'Saruman!' he cried, and his voice grew in power and authority. 'Behold, I am not Gandalf the Grey, whom you betrayed. I am Gandalf the White, who has returned from death. You have no colour now, and I cast you from the order and from the Council.'

> He raised his hand, and spoke slowly in a clear cold voice. 'Saruman, your staff is broken.' There was a crack, and the staff split asunder in Saruman's hand, and the head of it fell down at Gandalf's feet. 'Go!' said Gandalf. With a cry Saruman fell back and crawled away. (*TT*, III, x)

Saruman will not willingly admit to his wrongdoing, repent, and surrender his staff, so Gandalf unveils himself, revealing the new reality with which Saruman must account. He strips Saruman of his rank, his position, his power, and in doing so effects a permanent change in his body to match the change in his soul.[8] In Tolkien's work outer appearance matches inner

---

[7] We must acknowledge here that this opportunity comes with conditions. Saruman must surrender Orthanc and his staff (the mark of his position as an Istari to which he no longer has the right). So the freedom is simply the freedom to leave, not to continue on as he had been.

[8] Tolkien's description here of Saruman crawling away is suggestive of the

reality, and so when the characters next encounter Saruman he is utterly changed. His appearance reflects the reality of his soul, but because the change has only recently occurred, his outer manifestation does not yet fully reflect the dysformed soul within. Instead, he merely looks like a surly old beggar. After Saruman rejects the mercy offered to him one final time Gandalf comments on the change in Saruman saying, 'I fear nothing more can be made of him. He has withered altogether. All the same [...] I fancy he could do some mischief still in a small mean way' (*RK*, VI, vi). Petty meanness is all that is left to Saruman. There are no more grand schemes for world domination or mass subjugation. There is no more setting himself up, in Treebeard's words, as a Power (*TT*, III, iv). He has withered altogether, in body and in soul, and no great acts are left for him.

Yet even this lessened stature will fall away. He has made his choice and will follow it to the bitter end. Saruman then goes to the Shire to ruin and destroy, if he can, what was good and pure. He goes to exercise his petty vengeance upon those he perceives to have wronged him, expanding his dysformative community within the Shire, subjecting and subtly dominating its people. The dysformative community Saruman makes draws out the ugliness and death resident within its members. As we will see at the conclusion of Saruman's story, death has slowly been at work within him for decades, claiming ever more of him as he descends further into wickedness and sin.

As the Hobbits walk through their now devastated, but not ruined, homeland they see the results of Saruman's fall. The

---

depths to which Saruman will fall. It hints at his continued descent. The image is suggestive of a dog slinking away with its tail between its legs.

random, senseless destruction of the land reveals that Saruman has lost even the last shreds of his humanity, and descended to the level of a mere beast, or worse, an Orc. This is, in fact, the true state of his soul: it is thoroughly orkish.

After Saruman's death at the hands of his one remaining companion, the depths of his descent are revealed.[9] In one of the most striking passages in the whole of *The Lord of the Rings* the Hobbits witness Saruman's soul leaving his body as 'a grey mist […] rising slowly to a great height like smoke from a fire' (*RK*, VI, viii). It looks to the West, to the land from whence it came, but 'out of the West came a cold wind, and it bent away, and with a sigh dissolved into nothing' (*RK*, VI, viii). Saruman's soul is here rejected by those who sent him to Middle-earth and his passage back to the uncorrupted lands is denied. As Tolkien elsewhere describes it, 'his spirit went whithersoever it was doomed to go, and to Middle-earth, whether naked or embodied, came never back' (*UT*, p. 391). But the revelation of his soul's true state also reveals the corruption of his body. Frodo looks away from Saruman's rejected and dispersed spirit to the body before him 'with pity and horror, for as he looked it seemed that long years of death were suddenly revealed in it' (*RK*, VI, viii). Fleshly decay mirrors his barren soul. Outer appearance at last matches inner reality.

While his descent from Istari to beast represents a real loss, Saruman's true loss runs deeper still. It is not descent down the chain of being that matters most; it is the lost relationships and capacities. Saruman begins as one who can experience

---

[9] For a brief but lucid treatment of this final descent, see Germaine Paulo Walsh, 'Philosophic Poet: J.R.R. Tolkien's Modern Response to an Ancient Quarrel', in *Tolkien Among the Moderns*, ed. by Ralph C. Wood (Notre Dame: University of Notre Dame Press, 2015), pp. 7–49 (particularly pp. 27–28).

relationship and empower community, but ends as one who breaks communities and cuts himself off from others so fully that he becomes no-one and no-thing. He loses his access to euformative fellowship and loses his immortality and himself in the process.[10]

Frodo

Frodo's journey is a very different one: we witness his growth and transformation every step of the way. We see him at the beginning: a typical hobbit, enjoying the comforts of his stable and prosperous life, without any grand ambitions, but still longing for something more. We see him agree to take the Ring on a perilous journey, to leave friends and comforts behind, to renounce his place in the world in exchange for uncertainty, fear, and loss. We see him suffering under the burden of the Ring, and we see this suffering cause a light to grow steadily stronger within him. We see him stagger onward as the Ring grows heavier—with a spiritual weight that bears physical reality—as it exerts Sauron's will against his own. We see Frodo briefly unveiled, the outer matching the inner for a few moments (*TT*, IV, i and *RK*, VI, iii), as his inner brightness shines out in contrast to Gollum's shrunken, shadowy self. We

---

[10] We must qualify that his spirit remains immortal, though in the context of the story and of Arda itself it has perished and gone whithersover it was doomed to go. The Ainur who entered Eä 'must bide in it till the End, being involved in Time, the series of events that complete it' (*Letters*, p. 284). As Tolkien observes elsewhere, 'The indestructibility of *spirits* with free wills, even by the Creator of them, is also an inevitable feature, if one either believes in their existence, or feigns it in a story' (*Letters*, p. 280). So Saruman's spirit remains immortal as all created spirits must, but within the confines of Arda it is no more.

see the malevolent will of the Ring finally overcome him at the Cracks of Doom as he claims it—or, worse yet, is claimed by it. We see him after his eucatastrophic success, 'pale and worn, and yet himself again; and in his eyes there was peace now, neither strain of will, nor madness, nor any fear' (*RK*, VI, iii). We see him during the scouring of the Shire: grown, not in body like Merry and Pippin but, in spirit. And Saruman sees it too.

After Saruman tries to murder Frodo, Frodo commands everyone to let Saruman be, saying,

> 'He was great once, of a noble kind that we should not dare to raise our hands against. He is fallen, and his cure is beyond us; but I would still spare him, in the hope that he may find it'.
> (*RK*, VI, viii)

Where Saruman has become so dysformed that he cannot see Gandalf for what he has become, Frodo's euformation has empowered him to see Saruman for what he once was. Saruman then looks at Frodo with 'mingled wonder and respect and hatred' saying, 'You have grown, Halfling [...] Yes, you have grown very much' (*RK*, VI, viii). Frodo's pity for Saruman's fall presents a stark contrast to Frodo's words at the beginning when he says of Gollum, 'What a pity that Bilbo did not stab that vile creature, when he had a chance!' (*FR*, I, ii).

Pity is the significant term here, one with 'moral and imaginative worth' for Tolkien (*Letters*, p. 191), and it is used, particularly when capitalized, to communicate the kind of interaction that 'restrain[s] one from doing something immediately desirable and seemingly advantageous' (*Letters*, p. 191). It is marked not only by sorrow for the low estate of another, but also by a desire for the other's good to be achieved. It is a theologically grounded way of being in the world only embodied by the noble or ennobled, and as such it is fiercely opposed to Saruman's cruelty, indifference, spite, and inhumanity. As Saruman descends he loses the capacity for pity, disregarding others 'except as far as they serve him for the moment' (*TT*, III, iv). However, as Frodo ascends, his capacity to experience and express pity increases. Euformation is characterized by the capacity to reach out in Pity to those brought low by their dysformative journeys.

In the end, it is Pity 'that ultimately allows the Quest to be achieved' (*Letters*, p. 191). Frodo's capacity to express Pity flows out of his euformative journey of self-sacrifice and renunciation. In the end, the Shire is saved, but not for him. As Frodo says, 'It must often be so, Sam, when things are in danger: someone has to give them up, lose them, so that others may keep them' (*RK*, VI, ix). Frodo gives them up so Sam and his family can keep them. He has paid the price, but his reward awaits beyond the walls of the world where:

> at last on a night of rain Frodo smelled a sweet fragrance on the air and heard the sound of singing [...] over the water. And then it seemed to him that [...] the grey rain-curtain turned all to silver glass and was rolled back, and he beheld white shores and beyond them a far green country under a swift sunrise. (*RK*, VI, ix)

Works Consulted

Drout, Michael D.C., ed., *J.R.R. Tolkien Encyclopedia: Scholarship and Critical Assessment* (London: Routledge, 2007)

Fimi, Dimitra, *Tolkien, Race, and Cultural History: From Fairies to Hobbits* (Basingstoke: Palgrave Macmillan, 2009)

Walsh, Germaine Paulo, 'Philosophic Poet: J.R.R. Tolkien's Modern Response to an Ancient Quarrel', in *Tolkien Among the Moderns*, ed. by Ralph C. Wood (Notre Dame: University of Notre Dame Press, 2015), pp. 7–49

Zimbardo, Rose A., 'Moral Vision in The Lord of the Rings', in *Understanding The Lord of the Rings: The Best of Tolkien Criticism*, ed. by Rose A. Zimbardo and Neil D. Isaacs (Boston: Houghton Mifflin, 2004), pp. 68–75

'Tears are the very wine of blessedness': joyful sorrow in J.R.R. Tolkien's *The Lord of the Rings*

I have to confess that I am addressing this topic with some trepidation. In my previous work on J.R.R. Tolkien's legendarium, I have focused on exploring his socio-cultural context to illuminate the place of his work within contemporary intellectual history; or I have approached his work through his creative adaptation of medieval sources or more recent folklore to examine his particular use of the fantastic; or, elsewhere, I have attempted to elicit a theory of fantasy from Tolkien's self-reflective works, most importantly his essay 'On Fairy-Stories'.[1] But this essay is different in that I will attempt a reading of particular scenes in *The Lord of the Rings* which seem to me to hinge upon religious or theological premises.

There is, of course, a long tradition of Christian readings of Tolkien.[2] I have nothing against them—though I often find them more focused on using Tolkien to sermonize or preach,

---

[1] For example, Dimitra Fimi, *Tolkien, Race and Cultural History: From Fairies to Hobbits* (Basingstoke: Palgrave Macmillan, 2008); Dimitra Fimi, '"Mad Elves" and "Elusive Beauty": Some Celtic Strands of Tolkien's Mythology', *Folklore*, 117, 2 (2006), 156–70; Dimitra Fimi, 'Tolkien's "'Celtic' Type of Legends": Merging Traditions', *Tolkien Studies*, 4 (2007), 51–71; Dimitra Fimi, 'Tolkien and the Fantasy Tradition', in *Critical Insights: The Fantastic*, ed. by Claire Whitehead (CA: Salem Press, 2012), pp. 40–60.

[2] For an overview see Bradley J. Birzer, 'Christian Readings Of Tolkien', in *J.R.R. Tolkien Encyclopedia: Scholarship and Critical Assessment*, ed. by Michael D.C. Drout (New York: Routledge, 2006), pp. 99–101.

rather than on actually attempting to offer a critical appreciation of Tolkien's work. At the same time, I too have touched on some theological ideas in my book on Tolkien; though these tended to be rather eccentric or marginal theological ideas that linked Victorian Catholicism with fairies and fairylore.[3] And, it is such a—maybe not quite eccentric—but obscure idea from Christian theology that I will draw upon in this essay in an attempt to offer a different interpretation to Tolkien's work.

Let me begin with the essay I mentioned above: Tolkien's 'On Fairy-Stories'. In this essay, Tolkien declared that the function of fairy-tales was to provide fantasy, recovery, escape and consolation (*OFS*, p. 59). He elaborated on each of these four purposes, but the one he expanded on more, and with which I will be mainly concerned in this essay, is the last one: consolation, and especially 'the Consolation of the Happy Ending' (*OFS*, p. 75). Tolkien argued that a happy ending is an essential element of fairy-tales, and he coined a new term for it: 'eucatastrophe'. He claimed that 'all complete fairy-stories must have it' (*OFS*, p. 75), and further explained it by comparing it to drama. He wrote:

> Tragedy is the true form of Drama, its highest function; but the opposite is true of Fairy-story. Since we do not appear to possess a word that expresses this opposite—I will call it *Eucatastrophe*. The *eucatastrophic* tale is the true form of fairy-tale, and its highest function. The consolation of fairy-stories, the joy of the happy ending: or more correctly of the good catastrophe, the sudden joyous 'turn' […] is a sudden and miraculous grace: never to be counted on to recur. It does not deny the existence of *dyscatastrophe*, of sorrow

---

[3] Fimi, *Tolkien, Race and Cultural History*, pp. 40–61.

and failure: the possibility of these is necessary to the joy of deliverance; it denies (in the face of much evidence, if you will) universal final defeat and in so far is *evangelium*, giving a fleeting glimpse of Joy, Joy beyond the walls of the world, poignant as grief. (*OFS*, p. 75)

Tolkien does not use *evangelium* in this context only in its classical Greek sense: 'good news' (i.e. the sudden 'good turn' of the fairy-stories, the 'good news' of the happy ending); he also uses the word in its Hellenistic Greek meaning: 'gospel'. The importance of Christianity, and specifically Roman Catholicism, in Tolkien's life cannot—of course—be underestimated. However, in 'On Fairy-Stories' he went on to make a rather bold statement: he claimed that the Gospels contained a fairy-story, the greatest fairy-story of all, which 'embraces all the essence of fairy-stories' (*OFS*, p. 78). He claimed that:

The Birth of Christ is the eucatastrophe of Man's history. The Resurrection is the eucatastrophe of the story of the Incarnation. This story begins and ends in joy. (*OFS*, p. 78)

This joy is not just the ephemeral joy of this world. In the previous quotation Tolkien described it as 'Joy beyond the walls of the world, poignant as grief'. In a letter to his son Christopher a few years later, he elaborated on the nature of that joy by writing that:

Resurrection was the greatest 'eucatastrophe' possible in the greatest Fairy Story—and produces that essential emotion: Christian joy which produces tears because it is qualitatively so like sorrow, because it comes from those places where Joy

and Sorrow are at one, reconciled, as selfishness and altruism
are lost in Love. (*Letters*, p. 100)

Tolkien here seems to echo ideas on the real Christian joy, the
joy of God as opposed to the joy of the world. John's gospel
refers to the 'complete' joy that only Christ can give,[4] and in
Christ's own words in Mathew and John's gospels we hear that:
'Blessed are those who mourn, for they will be comforted',[5] and
'you will have pain, but your pain will turn into joy'.[6] Tolkien's
claim voices the same Christian argument: that in this world we
only feel profound sorrow, because real, profound joy, is not to
be found but in Christ's presence, it is not to be found but in
heaven, and we only get glimpses of it during our lives.

Tolkien's own 'fairy-stories' do include moments of
eucatastrophe as he described it, moments where—beyond all
hope—a sudden joyful turn occurs. In *The Hobbit* the most
poignant such moment is the coming of the Eagles that marks the
turn of the Battle of Five Armies and the victory of the forces of
good against the forces of evil (*Hobbit*, chapter 17). In *The Lord
of the Rings* there are more such instances: the sudden return of
Gandalf to the aid of the peoples of Middle-earth when he was
thought to be dead (*TT*, III, v); the destruction of Isengard by
the Ents, triggered by Merry and Pippin's accidental arrival to
Fangorn Forest (*TT*, III, ix); Sam's realisation that Frodo was
just wounded by the giant spider Shelob, and not killed (*RK*,
VI, i); and the arrival of the infantry of the Rohirrim in Gondor
during its siege (*RK*, V, iv). Indeed, Tolkien himself referred to
this latter joyous scene as one that moved him most profoundly

---

[4] John 15. 11.

[5] Matthew 5. 4.

[6] John 16. 20.

186

(*Letters*, p. 221).

Perhaps the most potent such scene is the moment when Sam wakes up in Gondor after the destruction of the Ring and finds out from Gandalf that he and Frodo are not dead, that Sauron is destroyed and that Middle-earth is saved. Tolkien's word choice to describe Sam's feelings in that instance is characteristic.

[...] he laughed and the sound was like music, or like water in a parched land; and as he listened the thought came to Sam that he had not heard laughter, the pure sound of merriment, for days upon days without count. It fell upon his ears like the echo of all the joys he had ever known. But he himself burst into tears. Then, as a sweet rain will pass down a wind of spring and the sun will shine out the clearer, his tears ceased, and his laughter welled up, and laughing he sprang from his bed. (*RK*, V, iv)

The same feeling is reproduced once more further on in the story, in even more emotive diction, when Frodo and Sam are taken to the feast of Gondor, and are praised as heroes. A minstrel sings a song of the destruction of the Ring, praising them as the ring-bearers and the reaction of Sam is the following:

And when Sam heard that he laughed aloud for sheer delight, and he stood up and cried: 'O great glory and splendour! And all my wishes have come true!' And then he wept.

And all the host laughed and wept, and in the midst of their merriment and tears the clear voice of the minstrel rose like silver and gold, and all men were hushed. And he sang to them, now in the Elven-tongue, now in the speech of the West,

> until their hearts, wounded with sweet words, overflowed, and
> their joy was like swords, and they passed in thought out to
> regions where pain and delight flow together and tears are the
> very wine of blessedness. (*RK*, V, iv)

This is probably the most characteristic passage in *The Lord of the Rings*, where joy and sorrow seem to blend and the word choice itself seems to underline this feeling: 'hearts […] wounded with sweet words', 'joy […] like swords', 'tears are the very wine of blessedness'. Tolkien seems to be following faithfully his own theory of 'eucatastrophe' in his fairy-tale and to comply with what he himself describes as the 'highest function of fairy-stories', the unexpected joyful ending that brings tears.

And here is the point that gave me pause when I first read *The Lord of the Rings*, and which I have continued to stop and ponder about every time I read it again. Sorrow mixed with joy, tears alongside laughter, sweetness that can wound—a series of paradoxes that ought not to be together, but which seem to belong quite naturally together in the text. What is going on here? Are we still in the realms of the degree of profundity that such emotions can cause? Is joy compared to pain because in this 'fallen' world pain is a much more familiar and potent feeling to compare with the sort of 'joy' that we can only reach in heaven?

What these questions, and these two extracts from *The Lord of the Rings*, have brought to my mind, is a rather obscure theological idea, much more current today in the Eastern Orthodox tradition rather than the Western Church: the concept of 'charmolypi' (χαρμολύπη). The word is a compound of the words 'χαρά' (joy) and 'λύπη' (sorrow) and can be translated

188

either as 'joyful sorrow' or 'sorrowful joy'—it's difficult to be precise, and actually the point is that the translation should not be precise: joy and sorrow blend seamlessly. The term was coined by St John Climacus, or St John Sinaites, a seventh-century Christian monk at the monastery on Mount Sinai. Having lived before the Great Schism—i.e. before the separation of the Church into East and West—he is revered as a saint by both the Roman Catholic and the Eastern Orthodox Churches.

St John Climacus extolled the 'positive character of spiritual tears':[7] in this theological view, tears are blessed because they earn passage—via repentance—from sin and death towards resurrection and the 'real' joy of Christ. St John actually seems to be more favourable towards those who have sinned and then repent through tears and mourning, eventually tasting the joy of redemption, rather than those that neither sin nor mourn:

> It seems to me that those who have fallen and are penitent are more blessed than those who have never fallen and who do not have to mourn over themselves, because through having fallen, they have pulled themselves up by a sure resurrection.[8]

Those who have sinned and mourn, and are saved via their repentance, have tasted something very similar to Christ's death and resurrection. They have fallen and have risen again. Interestingly, this idea of 'charmolypi' is particularly evoked

---

[7] Kallistos Ware, 'Introduction', in John Climacus, *The Ladder of Divine Ascent*, trans. by Colm Luibheid and Norman Russell (London: SPCK, 1982), pp. 1–70 (p. 26).

[8] John Climacus, *The Ladder of Divine Ascent*, trans. by Colm Luibheid and Norman Russell (London: SPCK, 1982), p. 128.

189

in the Orthodox tradition during Easter-time, especially on Saturday after Good Friday, when the excessive mourning for the crucified Christ is slowly giving way to the hope of joyful resurrection.

These elements seem to me to chime quite strongly with the scene of joyful tears and wounding sweetness in *The Lord of the Rings*, on the day after the Ring is destroyed. Tom Shippey has shown that Tolkien's choice of date for the destruction of the Ring—25 March—which becomes the end of the Third Age and the beginning of a new era for Middle-earth, was not accidental. The twenty-fifth of March is associated with the feast of the Annunciation, but in medieval tradition it was also considered the day of the crucifixion, Good Friday.[9] Sam's profound expression of 'charmolypi' therefore, his expression of 'joyful sorrow' or 'sorrowful joy', takes place the day after the destruction of the Ring, the point when the anticipation of the resurrection still blends with the sorrow of the crucifixion. And, indeed, the days that follow usher a new king in Gondor and a new age of Middle-earth, just as the resurrection of Christ is the end of the story of the gospels and the beginning of the Church.

What is more, St John's preference for sinners whose redemption may be given more profound meaning than the 'goodness' of those who do not sin, is—for me—another link between the unexpectedness and the miraculous-ness of Tolkien's 'eucatastrophe'. It is crucial for Tolkien that the final 'joyous turn' is sudden and unexpected. That there is a hesitation, rather than an entitlement, for a resolution.

---

[9] T.A. Shippey, *The Road to Middle-earth* (London: HarperCollins, 2005), p. 227.

In the same letter to Christopher that I quoted above, Tolkien tried to explain the importance of this hesitation, by recounting the story of a modern miracle at Lourdes he heard during a sermon:

> [...] the most moving story [was that] of the little boy with tubercular peritonitis who was not healed, and was taken sadly away in the train by his parents, practically dying with 2 nurses attending him. As the train moved away it passed within sight of the [Lourdes] Grotto. The little boy sat up. 'I want to go and talk to the little girl'—in the same train there was a little girl who had been healed. And he got up and walked there and played with the little girl; and then he came back, and he said 'I'm hungry now'. And they gave him cake and two bowls of chocolate and enormous potted meat sandwiches, and he ate them! [...] But at the story of the little boy [...] with its apparent sad ending and then its sudden unhoped-for happy ending, I was deeply moved [...] (*Letters*, p. 100)

One could be very cynical and say that all of this is, really, about emotional manipulation. About convincing the reader or listener of a story that all will end in tragedy, when suddenly everything is resolved, and the temporary loss of hope makes the moment of resolution even stronger. Leading up to the destruction of the Ring we are led to believe that we cannot expect Frodo and Sam to be saved. Yes, they will complete the task, but surely they will die heroically in the process. Sam gets rid of his cooking equipment in recognition of this. The coming of the Eagles is as unexpected as it is in *The Hobbit*— our heart strings are pulled and when we rejoice with Sam to be awake and alive, and we see Sam and Frodo praised as saviours in Gondor, we also experience this eucatastrophic moment.

191

Literature can do that—it can produce bodily changes: goose bumps, tears, a quickening of the heart rate.

But I do not think this is Tolkien's narratological experiment. I think he is trying to reproduce in these scenes the emotion of the story with the little boy at Lourdes, this feeling of being 'deeply moved' by what Tolkien later in this letter calls 'a sudden glimpse of Truth' (Truth with a capital T)—a 'preview' of joy that we can only just about taste, and which blends with the grief and sorrow of its own impossibility, or rather improbability.

Because it is also important to remember that—despite these moments of 'charmolypi' at this climactic, eucatastrophic moment in *The Lord of the Rings*—the story does not end there. On the contrary, the bewildered reader, after having been moved by such scenes of joyful sorrow and sorrowful joy, is faced with the most frustratingly sad chapter: 'The Scouring of the Shire' (*RK*, VI, viii). The Hobbits, who have travelled in all Middle-earth, have taken part in great adventures, and have played an important role is saving their world, return to their own peaceful rural village, but find it spoiled by Saruman and his machines and red brick buildings. The idyllic, safe Shire has been marred and the Hobbits seem to come back to their worst nightmare, as pre-viewed by Sam in the mirror of Galadriel. The Hobbits have to start a new battle to restore the Shire to its original state and, at the same time, Frodo seems to be still affected by the painful power of the Ring.

Meanwhile, Middle-earth has been saved, but the Elves depart and leave it forever. Evil is destroyed but magic and enchantment is lost too. At the very end of the book, Frodo departs for Valinor, together with Gandalf and the Elves, to be healed, an 'Arthurian ending' (*Sauron Defeated*, p. 132) which can well be—of course—a euphemism for death. The last scene, where Sam, Merry and Pippin bid farewell forever to Frodo and Gandalf is full of sorrow and melancholy. Tolkien describes the Hobbits' sadness and Gandalf's reaction to it:

> But Sam was now sorrowful at heart, and it seemed to him that if the parting would be bitter, more grievous still would be the long road home alone. (*RK*, VI, ix)

And Gandalf said:

> Well, here at last, dear friends, on the shores of the Sea comes the end of our fellowship in Middle-earth. Go in peace! I will not say: do not weep; for not all tears are an evil. (*RK*, VI, ix)

Here, however, Gandalf refers to real grief, real tears, not that blend of joy and sorrow Tolkien seems to define as crucial to eucatastrophe.

The reader of *The Lord of the Rings* is thus left with a bitter taste at the end of the book. The same pattern can be observed in *The Hobbit*, albeit in a milder form: at the end of the book the dragon is killed and the battle won, but nevertheless Bilbo goes back to find his house practically robbed, and despite his adventures he has lost his reputation among his fellow Hobbits.

It is beyond the scope of this essay to go further into this 'spoiling' of eucatastrophe that Tolkien allows. I am sure we can all think of a number of reasons: some of them biographical (such as the tragedies of his early life with the death of his parents, or his traumatic experience at the Somme, where he lost dear friends, alongside an entire generation); others more associated with his spiritual or theological worldview of a 'fallen' world, in which we live to fight 'the long defeat'. What I hope to have managed, is to convince readers to linger for a little longer on those passages of 'charmolypi', the moments of 'eucatastrophe', which are not moments of triumph and excessive rejoicing, but rather more subtle moments of blended joy and sorrow, offering—perhaps—a preview of the 'real' joy of Paradise.

Works Consulted

Birzer, Bradley J., 'Christian Readings Of Tolkien', in *J.R.R. Tolkien Encyclopedia: Scholarship and Critical Assessment*, ed. by Michael D.C. Drout (New York: Routledge, 2006), pp. 99–101

Fimi, Dimitra, *Tolkien, Race and Cultural History: From Fairies to Hobbits* (Basingstoke: Palgrave Macmillan, 2008)

——, '"Mad Elves" and "Elusive Beauty": Some Celtic Strands of Tolkien's Mythology', *Folklore*, 117, 2 (2006), 156–70

——, 'Tolkien's "'Celtic' Type of Legends": Merging Traditions', *Tolkien Studies*, 4 (2007), 51–71

——, 'Tolkien and the Fantasy Tradition', in *Critical Insights: The Fantastic*, ed. by Claire Whitehead (CA: Salem Press, 2012), pp. 40–60

John Climacus, *The Ladder of Divine Ascent*, trans. by Colm Luibheid and Norman Russell (London: SPCK, 1982)

Shippey, T.A., *The Road to Middle-earth* (London: HarperCollins, 2005)

Ware, Kallistos 'Introduction', in John Climacus, *The Ladder of Divine Ascent*, trans. by Colm Luibheid and Norman Russell (London: SPCK, 1982), pp. 1–70

About the Contributors

Gaëlle Abaléa teaches English at a high school in Orléans while working on a PhD on death and immortality in Tolkien's work. Her master's degree at Paris-Sorbonne University dealt with Christian myths in Tolkien's legendarium. She participated in *L'encyclopédie du Hobbit*, edited by Pré au Clercs and published in 2013. She is a member of the French association Tolkiendil.

Tânia Azevedo is a PhD student from Instituto de Letras e Ciências Humanas, Minho University, in Braga, Portugal and is developing her work on the medieval text *Sir Gawain and the Green Knight*. She has a four-year degree in Modern Languages and Literature—Portuguese and English Studies from Faculty of Arts, University of Lisbon (2003). After that, she completed a two-year degree in Education to teach Portuguese and English in schools (2005). Her master's degree was also completed in Lisbon (2009) in English Literature, where she explored the re-writing of the Christian myth in the works of J.R.R. Tolkien.

Aslı Bülbül Candaş was born in 1988 in İstanbul. In 2004, she started studying English Language and Literature at İstanbul University. She graduated in 2009 and worked as a translator and English teacher in various companies and schools. In August 2013, she started to work in İstanbul Aydın University in the Applied English-Turkish Translation department as an academic, and completed her master's degree in English Language and Literature in 2016.

Giovanni Carmine Costabile holds an MPhil in Philosophy from the Università della Calabria in Italy. Prior work experiences include journalism and different artistic endeavours, including the publication of a collection of his love-poems, **Lingue di te**, in Italy in 2017, and his contribution to street-theatre performance, wall painting and the creation of costumes, masks and props for the 2011 Halloween Shandon Parade in Cork, Ireland. Already a big fan of Tolkien as a teenager, at the moment he is working as a private teacher and a freelance translator, while researching and publishing as an independent scholar, including forthcoming publications in the *Inklings Jahrbuch* and in the journal of *Tolkien Studies*.

Dr Dimitra Fimi is a senior lecturer in English at Cardiff Metropolitan University. Her monograph *Tolkien, Race and Cultural History* (Palgrave Macmillan, 2008) won the Mythopoeic Scholarship Award for Inklings Studies and she co-edited the critical edition of Tolkien's *A Secret Vice* (HarperCollins, 2016) which won The Tolkien Society Award for Best Book. She lectures on Tolkien, fantasy, children's literature and medievalism. Her latest monograph, *Celtic Myth in Contemporary Children's Fantasy*, appeared from Palgrave Macmillan in 2017. Other recent work includes chapters in *A Companion to J.R.R. Tolkien* (Blackwell, 2014), and *Revisiting Imaginary Worlds: An Subcreation Studies Anthology* (Routledge, 2016). She has contributed articles for the TLS and The Conversation, and appears regularly on BBC Radio Wales.

Daniel Helen is an officer without portfolio and trustee of The Tolkien Society. Elected in 2014, he is mainly responsible for the Society's digital operations, including its website. He holds a Bachelor of Arts degree in history from the University of Southampton and a Master of Studies degree in medieval history from the University of Oxford, where his research focused on the development of law and government in England from the Anglo-Saxon period until the end of the thirteenth century.

Dr Andrew Higgins is a Tolkien scholar who specialises in exploring the role of language invention in fiction. His thesis 'The Genesis of Tolkien's Mythology' (which he is currently preparing for publication) explored the interrelated nature of myth and language in Tolkien's earliest work. He is also the co-editor (with Dr Dimitra Fimi) of *A Secret Vice: Tolkien on Invented Languages* published by HarperCollins in April 2016. Andrew has also taught an online course on language invention for Signum University/Mythgard Institute. Andrew has been a member of The Tolkien Society since 2007. He is also director of development at Glyndebourne Opera in Sussex.

Massimiliano Izzo currently lives in Oxford, where he is employed as a research software engineer at the University of Oxford. He enjoys reading speculative fiction and all kinds of folklore literature, and listening to a lot of good old heavy metal. Among his other interests there are exploring the relationship between genre and literary fiction, all sorts of conspiracy theories, and backpacking around the globe.

Dr Irina Metzler is a leading expert on cultural, religious and social aspects of physical disability in the European Middle Ages. In her first book-length study of the topic, she has combined the approaches of modern disability studies with historical sources to investigate the intellectual framework within which medieval cultures positioned physically impaired persons. A second monograph on social and economic conditions of medieval disability followed, with a third book on intellectual disability in the Middle Ages completing the trilogy. Her wider research interests revolve around medieval notions of history and the past, perceptions of the natural world in the Middle Ages (in particular cats as ambiguous animals), and historical anthropology, topics on which she has published a number of articles in both English and German journals.

Anna Milon is a student of medieval literature with a BA from Royal Holloway, University of London, currently undertaking an MA at the University of York. She has been a member of The Tolkien Society since 2014, and a member of the committee since March 2016. Her research interests include folklore, medieval animals and modern fantasy writing. In her free time, Anna is the proud owner of a ginger cat called Sherlock, an archer (longbow) and an amateur HEMA sword fighter (longsword and messer).

Matthew B. Rose received his BA (History and English) and MA (Systematic Theology) degrees from Christendom College. He teaches Religion and History at Bishop O'Connell High School in Arlington, Virginia (USA). Matthew also runs *Quidquid Est, Est!*, a Catholic Q&A blog, lectures on a variety of topics, and writes regularly for numerous online publications, including *Catholic Exchange*, *Those Catholic Men*, and *Homiletic & Pastoral Review*. He and his family live in Falls Church, Virginia.

Sarah Rose, originally from California, has been an avid fan of Tolkien since she was 10. In 2008, she earned her BA degree in Philosophy from Christendom College in Virginia. Her thesis examined the connection between music and creation in the myths of Tolkien and C.S. Lewis, in the philosophies of Plato, Pythagoras, Plotinus, and Thomas Aquinas, and in the creation account in the book of Genesis. She and her husband Matthew currently live in Virginia with their two sons.

Adam B. Shaeffer is a PhD candidate in Durham University's Department of Theology and Religion where he is researching models of spiritual formation in Tolkien's legendarium, with particular emphasis on The Lord of the Rings. Prior to studying at Durham, he earned MA degrees in Spiritual Formation and Classroom Instruction from Talbot School of Theology and Biola University respectively.

Index

Lightning Source UK Ltd.
Milton Keynes UK
UKHW02f1445120318
319195UK00002BA/77/P